God, You Must Have Me Confused with Someone Else:

Seeing What I Was Missing

Bob Konopa, O.F.M.

To—
Emma

Fr. Bob Konopa ofm.

God, You Must Have Me Confused with Someone Else: Seeing What I Was Missing
Bob Konopa, O.F.M.

Book Design: Tau Publishing Design Dept.
Cover Design: Tau Publshing Design Dept.
Cover Photo: Donna Lasserre, Westside images, Brusly, LA
Image of Christ page 57: Hook's Head of Christ © Concordia
Publishing House, www.cph.org. All rights reserved. Used by
permission.

Editor: Mary Esther Stewart, SFO

For permission contact:
Tau Publishing, LLC
Permissions Dept.
1422 East Edgemont Avenue
Phoenix, AZ 85006

First Edition, October 2011
10 9 8 7 6 5 4 3 2 1

ISBN: 978-1-61956-007-9

Published by Tau Publishing, LLC
www.Tau-Publishing.com
Printed in the United States of America

Tau-Publishing.com
Words of Inspiration

CONTENTS

PART ONE

PART TWO

I dedicate this book to my parents,
Mr. & Mrs. Norbert and Martha Konopa,
shown here on their 70th anniversary of marriage,
August 27, 2011

With gratitude

To my family, especially my parents, Norbert and Martha Konopa, who achieved seventy years of marriage and created a wonderful home for us all.

To my Franciscan family, especially the Friars of the Assumption of the Blessed Virgin Mary Province, ofm-abvm.org, who formed in me a vocation of community and ministry.

To Tau-publishing, for their personal and professional guidance to transform my manuscript into this book.

To the many people who by their friendship, supported, encouraged and challenged me, especially those who helped me to see spiritually in a new way.

To my readers who helped edit this book, especially my cousin Janet for her skillful editing who, I was told, edits everything she reads.

To the anonymous people throughout the years who unknowingly said to me, "You should write a book." I finally listened and followed their advice.

Part One

God, who are You?
and
God, who am I?

St. Francis of Assisi

I always admired and marveled how anyone could write an entire book. Writing a book seemed overwhelming and foreign to me. When I thought about writing, I quickly concluded only authors could write books. I debated with God, "Remember back in college how I struggled with my Introductory Writing course?"

However, while I could not let go of this lingering idea to write, more importantly, *this idea would not let go of me.* I knew I could neither "live with myself" nor be at peace until I actually followed through. I felt somewhat like Jeremiah, the prophet. Jeremiah wanted to stop speaking about God. He wrote, "I would say to myself, 'I will not think about Him [God], I will not speak in His name anymore,' but then there seemed to be a fire burning in my heart, imprisoned in my bones. The effort to restrain it wearied me, I could not do it." (Jer. 20:9). Like Jeremiah, this would not let go of me.

If I could leave myself out of this book and stay

private, I would gladly do so. However, we are God's instruments. Through each of us, the compassion, love, faithfulness, forgiveness, justice, mercy, and peace of God becomes knowable, visible, concrete, heard, and experienced. We are the hands and feet, the eyes and ears, the voice, compassion, and justice of God; therefore, these challenging and somewhat haunting questions come to mind: If not through us, who? If not now, when?

I hope this book will be relevant for many people without regard to denomination, ethnic background, religious persuasion, color of skin, cultural background, age, gender, believer or nonbeliever. I hope there is something for everyone in this book. How is that for lofty goals, or maybe unrealistic goals, but why not aim high?

Allow me to introduce myself. I am a Franciscan priest in the Catholic Church. I professed my solemn vows with my Franciscan community in August of 1986. I was ordained a priest in June of 1991 and have primarily been involved with ministry in parishes. Having joined the Franciscan community when I was twenty-nine years old and ordained a priest at forty years old, I am referred to as a late vocation. However, I also say that while I am known as a late vocation, I was *right on time.*

I chose the vocation of religious life, and to live it as a Franciscan friar. The Franciscan Order is known as the Order of Friars Minor (O.F.M.), meaning the Order of Lesser Brothers. St. Francis of Assisi, the Italian founder of the Franciscan Order, wanted himself and his followers to consider themselves less than everyone to demonstrate humility and simplicity before God and others.

This book contains numerous true stories and experiences, events and happenings over the years that gradually helped me to "see" more clearly. I am eternally grateful for all I have learned, come to know and believe, and to see for the first time. Indeed, it was like putting on a new pair of eyeglasses and seeing what is already there, what is already true. What I have come to see, know, trust and believe is not because of what I did. It is through the grace and goodness of God, and the goodness of God at work in and through the events and people in my life.

CHAPTER 1

They Have Eyes but Do Not See

I am the youngest of six children, five boys and one girl. We all attended the same elementary school, Mill Creek School, which my Dad attended back in the 1920s. This school was a little one-room schoolhouse that served as a classroom for grades one through eight. Preschool and kindergarten were not offered at that time.

Mill Creek School, located in central Wisconsin, was a great place to start my education. The school was about one and one-half miles from my family's dairy farm. My brothers and sister and I either walked to school or rode our bikes. I attended Mill Creek School from first through sixth grade. For those entire six years, I had the same teacher. Thank goodness she was a great teacher! At the end of sixth grade, the school district closed my school. Instead of being able to attend a school only one and one-half miles from our farm, my new school was twelve miles from home and I had to ride a school bus for the first time.

While in fourth grade at Mill Creek School, the county nurse visited our school to check everyone's eyesight. This was the very first time my eyesight was checked. Before my eye test, I thought my eyesight was fine. But as soon as the nurse posted the eye chart on the wall, I knew immediately I was in trouble.

Unlike the contemporary eye charts with numbers and letters, this eye chart consisted of only one letter, the letter E. You are probably thinking, how hard can that be? The letter E appeared in different sizes and configurations. The letter appeared backwards, on its side, or upside down. All I had to say was "ceiling, floor, window or wall" to describe the direction to which the "E" pointed. I failed the test miserably.

The nurse advised me to see an optometrist in order to receive a more professional and thorough eye exam. She said I needed eyeglasses. I did not like the sound of that. I had to give in. What could I do? I was only in fourth grade. Needless to say, I failed the optometrist's eye test as well. He filled out a prescription and measured me for glasses. I wondered, what would this be like to wear glasses? Little did I realize or speculate at the time when I first put on those glasses that the glasses would symbolize something highly significant, meaningful, and even spiritual in my life, namely how I was seeing and not seeing.

A few weeks later, someone from the optometrist's office phoned that my glasses were ready to be picked up. When I put those glasses on for the first time, it felt so strange. The optometrist carefully looked around each ear and then the bridge of my nose to make sure the glasses fit properly. I thought I would never become accustomed to wearing glasses. No matter where I looked, I saw the menacing outline of rims and lenses. But once we got out of his office, and walked outside on the street, I could not believe what I was seeing and how I was seeing for the first time. As I rode in the car on the way back home to our farm, everything looked so much clearer, brighter, more colorful, distinct and brilliant.

We arrived at our farm and got out of our car to go into the house. As my mother walked toward the house to prepare a quick lunch, she told me that it would not take her long, so I should come in too. I told her, "In a little while." Wearing my new glasses, I walked and walked all around the back of our house, the front of our house, for I do not know how long. It was impossible to take it all in. For the first time everything looked so beautiful. It was almost overwhelming. I could not believe that this is the way the world looked to everyone else. I could not believe what I had been missing.

As I walked around our house and yard, I could not believe what I was seeing. I could not believe how I was seeing. I looked north to our neighbor's woods. The trees were various shades of green. Before my glasses, all I could see was a glob of green, the trees being undistinguishable from each other. I looked down. Our lawn was so green, too, and made up of *individual* blades of grass. I looked up. The sky was a blue that I never knew existed. I looked east in the direction of our neighbor's pond. I could actually see the pond from this distance for the first time. The water in our neighbor's pond sparkled and shimmered brilliantly beneath the bright sunshine. I saw a bird fly by. I could actually see its colors, where before it would have looked more like a blur darting through the air. I did not want to stop discovering this new world of color, this new world so beautiful, so spectacular. Though I did not want to go inside, lunch was ready.

Over time, looking back at this experience, I realized something so important, so significant. The world that I could see through these new eyeglasses was THERE ALL THE TIME. This world of color and beauty did not begin when I put my eyeglasses on for the first time. This world always existed, but without my glasses, I just could not see it. I needed something or someone besides myself to show me that I was not seeing as I could, and to help me to see.

Before my eye exam, I thought I was seeing fine. Before putting on my new eyeglasses, I had not realized what I had been missing. However, over the years I realize just how true this is, especially in a spiritual way. Today, when I see people so spiritually distant or apathetic, I understand their indifference but, at the same time, I want to say to them, "You have no idea what you are missing!"

CHAPTER 2

Lord, I Want to See!

I truthfully admit I do not know where I would be without certain people in my life. They may be people whom I know, and with whom I still remain in relationship, or people who have passed in and out of my life. These people helped me, showed me, and taught me to "see" what I was missing. A number of these people helped me to actually "see" spiritually with new eyes, that is, to see what I was missing. I needed someone or something to help me to see properly, to point out to me how I was not seeing clearly, or in some cases, to help me see what was already there. This type of seeing is all part of spiritual growth, growth in self-awareness, and growth as a healthy, well grounded human being.

I do not see as clearly as I would like, namely because I am fully aware that the more I see, the more I realize how much more there is that I still do not see. Similarly, the more I know, I realize how much more there is that I do not know. That is just the way it is, and that is okay. With the Lord there is always more to "see" and more to know. The Lord will always invite us on a path, a journey, to know, see and understand more deeply. When we walk with the Lord and allow the Lord to teach us, our Christian lives take on a feeling of adventure. Looking at our Christianity in this way, being a follower of Jesus is never boring.

Jesus is described in Scripture as a teacher. He still is a teacher and wants to teach us. As a Buddhist proverb states, "When the student is ready, the teacher will come." Maybe our task is simply to be ready, and to stay connected and open to the One who leads, guides, and teaches us. Much of the teaching of Jesus seems to come to us by means of life lessons and life experiences.

Putting on eyeglasses for the first time as a fourth grader, I learned that we all need someone or something besides ourselves to help us to see, not just physically, but to really see and understand more deeply. It takes considerable openness and self-honesty to admit that we do not see clearly, or at least that we need something or someone to help us. This help can come from personal relationships, Scripture, Church teaching, wisdom figures, personal and communal prayer, spiritual direction, spiritual reading, etc.

Jesus often said, "Let those who have eyes, let them see" (Matt 13:13-16). The Lord will continue to draw us deeper and deeper into relationship with Him, as far and as deep as we are willing to go. Through this relationship with the Lord, we will be given new ways to understand, and we will begin to see more deeply. A number of authors emphasize that spirituality and conversion are all about seeing, seeing God, others, our world, and ourselves more clearly. There is only one reality. The difference is how we see this reality. I often feel compelled to pray, "Lord, give me eyes to see as you see."

I found myself asking the Lord, "What do you want to teach me? What am I not seeing? What am I still blind to? Help me to see, as you see." Eventually a new, great and key question arose within me: "What does God *see in me* that I do not yet see? How can I see myself as God sees me?" Is this even possible? As I began to receive surprising and beautiful answers to this personal question that I posed to God, all I could say back to God in reply was, *"God, you must have me confused with someone else."* So much began to change, and it happened from the inside out. My "little world" began to burst open. My spiritual "seeing" progressed steadily and gradually. I knew I would and could never be the same. I had put on a new pair of eyeglasses, I was seeing through a new lens, I began to see anew for the first time. Through the grace and goodness of God, thanks be to God, I pray that this new seeing continues. I say, "Lord, give me new eyes to see. Lord, please do not stop teaching me."

CHAPTER 3

But That's Not Me

But, that's not me! "You must have me confused with someone else." There were times when this response made a lot of sense and saved me from embarrassment, and even some hurt and pain, whether physical or emotional. At times this response or self-perception is most truthful, sensible and wise. We are not always qualified, prepared, or able to participate in every activity or successfully accomplish a particular job because what is expected of us is beyond our ability or expertise.

In high school, for our physical education class each fall, we played football. Football should be fun. At the beginning of the class period, we would choose sides to make up the two teams. I was always the last, or if I was lucky, the second to last person picked by either team. I would watch as classmate after classmate was chosen, and then I would hear those familiar words spoken with disgust, "Aaaah, we'll take Konopa." What else could he do? I was the last one left standing there alone. Finally the two teams were ready. Let the game begin.

I particularly remember one cool fall morning. In the huddle, the quarterback looked my way and said, "We need another body on the line to block and to protect me."

What was he thinking? I know what I was thinking: "That is not me. You must have me confused with someone else." When we broke the huddle, and trotted up to the line, I felt like a real football player. But that feeling was short lived. I lined up against a much bigger body. Every *body* was bigger than mine. I was tall enough, five feet ten inches, but only one hundred thirty five pounds. I knew this was not going to turn out well.

I could only hope that the classmate lined up in front of me would have some mercy and just gently push me aside. Maybe he would graze by me like flicking a bug off one's arm, not smash or crush it to bits. No such luck. He obviously was unable to read my mind or interpret the terror written all over my face.

So, there I was, lined up against one of the better athletes of my class. Because I knew the play called was a pass, I had to block this athletic classmate who was eagerly poised to blow right past or through me. I do not remember a lot of what happened on that play, but I know that he could have hardly known I was even there as he cut his way to the quarterback. I suppose you could say I felt like I was run over by the proverbial Mack truck. I felt like he knocked me into tomorrow.

I got up off the ground and I stumbled back to the huddle for the next play. I had been knocked over but not knocked senseless, so I pleaded my case in the huddle, "Hey guys, that's not me. I am not the one who can block this guy." Mercifully, the quarterback sent me to the outside to line up as a wide receiver. As I think about it now, he probably realized I could not provide him any safety or protection anyway. I am sure he made the change only for his own good.

These responses, "You must have me confused with some else," or "But that is not me," can limit self-growth or even limit growth in the Spirit of God. After I graduated from high school, I did not want to go to school four more years, so I attended a vocational or technical school. Little did I know at that time that one day I would be a freshman beginning college at the age of twenty nine, and after college, pursue a four-year graduate degree in Theology.

After two years at the technical institute, I graduated with special honors and a two-year Associate Degree in Accounting. Before graduation, the dean of the technical institute called me to his office. He congratulated me for my successful academic achievements, asked me to represent my graduating class, and to give the speech at the graduation ceremony. My immediate thought was, you guessed it, *but that's not me; you must have me confused with someone else.* I declined his request. I am sure he was shocked when I turned down this honor. He asked another student who gladly accepted the offer. During the graduation ceremony, I felt relieved that I did not have to speak, but at the same time, I felt a bit self-defeated and always wondered what would have happened if I had accepted his offer.

This same self-defeating attitude plagued me at a young age. When I was in either second or third grade our church hosted a three-night parish mission. A visiting priest spoke to a packed church. I sat and listened to this priest who was dressed in a rather unusual looking garb. I was so taken in by him and his stories. I thought to myself, how great life would be if I could travel from church to church wearing some similar kind of garb, and talk about God and tell stories like he was doing? But immediately my next thought was, *"But that's not me."*

Bob Konopa
2nd Grade
Mill Creek School

CHAPTER 4

Awakening to a Personal God

After I graduated with my Associate Degree in Accounting, I worked as an accountant at two different jobs, each for five years. The first five years I worked as the office manager in an automobile dealership, and the following five years in a public accounting firm. Professionally, my life was in good shape. Everything seemed to be in place. I had a good secure accounting job, and I thoroughly enjoyed working for the owners and with my co-workers. Every income tax season, January through April, ushered in a new pace and volume of work. The normal number of hours doubled and sometimes tripled because of the additional demands of the tax season.

Every tax season, we all geared up for the avalanche of paperwork that poured into our office and eventually spilled out onto our desks. The owners were well aware of the seasonally expanded workload, and they hired additional part time workers for the tax season. One of the part-time workers profoundly affected my life, not professionally, but personally and spiritually.

She was a wife, mother and grandmother, and a delightful person to be around. Her sense of humor was wonderful and contagious. She was a great listener, and I was especially attracted to how peaceful and peace-filled she was. I enjoyed just being around her. She was joyful, optimistic, and welcoming. She freely expressed her faith and the importance that her faith held for her life. I envied all that.

I finally rustled up enough nerve or courage, I am not sure which, to sit and talk with her on a more personal level. I told her something was missing in my life and I needed to attend a Bible study or something more spiritual in nature. She said she attended a meeting every Tuesday night in the basement of her church. Though it was not a typical Bible study, probably like I would imagine a Bible study, nevertheless she said, "Keep an open mind and come next Tuesday night."

When Tuesday night rolled around, I drove to the church, and walked down into the basement. I heard from a distance a rather large and noisy number of people socializing. I quietly slipped into the crowd and hoped the meeting would start soon because I did not know anyone. I looked for my co-worker, but I did not see her. The chairs were arranged in a circular fashion, one row in front of the other configured something like the rings of a tree. I wanted to sit down as quickly as possible. Without thinking but only reacting, I sat on a chair in the inner circle. The meeting began. I was surrounded on all sides and behind me. I had no way to escape without making a scene. I was stuck for the entire meeting. I could not escape, and I had no place to hide.

The meeting began with music and song, with talented, spirited, and enthusiastic guitarists and song leaders. Though the songs were foreign to me, I thoroughly enjoyed the music as well as the upbeat and spirited atmosphere all around me. Did they ever sing! While I was surrounded by strangers, I gradually felt less and less like a stranger to them.

I was surrounded with song, with heartfelt prayer and praise to God, which I had never heard expressed so beautifully and personally. However, I felt nervous and uneasy as they openly and verbally praised God and, at times, in strange languages. I wondered if I belonged there. I did not know it at the time, but this was my first Charismatic prayer meeting. The prayer group leader led an inspiring Bible teaching and spoke on a personal and experiential level. The people were invited to share. They openly spoke about Jesus, again on such a personal level, and spoke about how the Scriptures influenced them and impacted their lives. I did not know what to make of it. It never occurred to me that Jesus could be this personal or be this personally known and present in one's life.

After the meeting, some people came to me, introduced themselves, asked me my name, and spontaneously hugged me. They did not know me. I did not know them. Hugs were scarce in my personal life. I did not know what to do with that. Still I was determined to walk out of that basement as quickly as I could after the meeting ended without drawing any attention to myself.

Finally, when I had reached what I thought was a "safe distance" from the meeting place, I turned toward the exit and walked really fast without making it look like I was running. I heard a voice coming from behind me rather loudly calling my name, "Bob, Bob, where are you going? Slow down!" I stopped as I recognized the voice as being that of my coworker. When she caught up with me, I told her that I did not belong here, and this prayer meeting was not what I had in mind when I asked her about a Bible study. She replied, "Remember, I said to keep an open mind. I did. I will see you tomorrow at work."

A week had gone by. It was Tuesday night again, and I had to make a decision. I paced the floor in my apartment trying to decide if I should go back to that church basement. Maybe, I reasoned, I could arrive just before the meeting started, sit in the outer row of the circle, and then quickly escape without much notice.

What I did not realize at the time, but I know now, is

that I returned that second Tuesday night for the fellowship, for the hugs. I did not want to miss those hugs and the friendliness of the people. Their friendliness was real, refreshingly authentic. I convinced myself that I should go back because, after all, I did enjoy the music, the singing, and the personal sharing. But most of all, whether I realized it or not, I did not want to miss being with those people. I returned, and I returned every Tuesday night.

I do not know what kind of opinion or experience, if any, you have regarding the Charismatic Renewal. Perhaps you were or are an active member, perhaps you are suspicious of the Renewal, perhaps you have no opinion or a negative opinion. For me, the Charismatic Renewal was a major means through which God became radically personal to me for the first time. For others, there are other means or ways. I have no intention and choose not to write about the pros and cons of the Charismatic Renewal. I only know that, through the Renewal and the people, I discovered a spiritual world that I did not know existed, a "world" that was there all the time, but I could not see it. I did not even know there was such a thing as spirituality.

As I look at my years with the Charismatic Renewal, I compare the Renewal to what happened to Eli and Samuel in 1 Sam. 3:1-21. Samuel was asleep, but a voice woke him. Samuel thought it was Eli, who called him. Samuel went to Eli and said, "Here I am." But Eli told Samuel that he did not call him, and that Samuel should go back to sleep. This happened three times. Eli eventually figured out that it was the Lord who called Samuel, the child. Samuel did not yet know the Lord, and the word of the Lord had not yet been revealed to him. I was like Samuel, and the Charismatic Renewal was my Eli. The people and spirituality of the Charismatic Renewal helped me to hear the Word of God, to believe that God is extremely personal, personally involved, and connected with my life rather than distant and remote.

Through the Charismatic Renewal I met so many good people, and I enjoyed my relationships with such friendly, fun-loving and God-loving people. I was very shy and reserved. It was hard for me to allow anyone to get to know the real me. I suppose you could say I did not even know myself. After one prayer meeting, a person introduced me to another saying, "I would like you to meet Bob." She continued, "He is an accountant, and he is really smart." Her introduction felt so hollow. I thought to myself, I am more than that! I am more than a smart accountant! Is this all they know about me? Is this all they see when they see me?" Is this all I allowed them to know about me? I am more than this!

I had always heard how God touched the lives of others, but unexpectedly, one night, it must have been "my turn" to discover and experience God's touch, God's presence. The leader of the prayer meeting invited us to open our Bibles to Romans, chapter 3, starting with verse 23. I did actually have a Bible with me but, of course, I had to sneak a peek at the table of contents to find where Romans was located. The leader began to read, "All have sinned and fallen short of the glory of God. Yet all are equally justified by the free gift of his grace through being set free in Christ Jesus."

In the leader's discussion of this passage, she said, "When God looks at us, God sees Jesus. God sees one of His own, a Beloved son or daughter, a Beloved child." It was not only what she said, but also how she said this that really got my attention. She spoke with such joy, excitement and sincerity. She had a big smile on her face! I started to feel something happening inside of me. I became emotional, and I did not know what to do. I did not know if I could trust this feeling or not. What was happening within me?

Something inside of me was being freed and good news was flooding in. Tears started to well up; I instinctively tried hard to hide my emotions, and yet, at the same time, I did not want the tears to stop. A crusty shell was cracking open completely beyond my control. I felt loved and accepted. I felt forgiven. I felt like I was one with everyone there. All have sinned. When God looks at us, God sees Jesus. Oh my gosh! What do I do with this? How do I deserve this? Her message seemed too good to be true! When something seems too good to be true, is that when we tap into grace? Is that when we are touched by grace? Can this be true? My tears told me it is true, it is so.

The meeting ended and it was time to go, time to make my usual quick, quiet and solitary escape. But this time I did not want to leave. I was not the same person I was when I first walked into the room when the meeting began. I did not want to disappear like I usually did. I wanted to hug everyone in that room. Something in me had cracked open, and I loved every minute of it. Whatever it was, I silently prayed to God, "Don't stop doing this!" It had to be God, right? "Whatever you are doing God, I want more! God, don't stop."

For the first time in my life, I felt connected with God on a personal level. This relationship between the Lord and myself was a real relationship, a two-way relationship. I had actually related in a <u>personal</u> way to a Scripture passage during a Bible teaching! Scripture had come alive for me! I will always remember that Scripture passage, what happened to me, and I will always be thankful that God's truth and grace touched me that night.

This passage and teaching from Romans brought into question so many thoughts and assumptions that I held, whether or not I was consciously aware of them. This passage clearly stated that ALL have sinned and fallen short of the glory of God. ALL includes me. I did not have to be perfect in order to be acceptable to God or to myself. I could not be perfect anyway. It was impossible to be perfect. To be human is to be imperfect. It was good to be human.

It is God's free gift of grace that brings us into a relationship with Him. It did not all depend on me! When God looks at us, God sees Jesus; God sees one of His own Beloved sons or daughters. It seems too good to be true. Through that Scripture passage, truth was spoken. When truth meets our untruth, healing can happen, and sometimes healing is revealed through tears.

After that night, I knew I wanted more and more of this personal intimacy with God as quickly as I could. I started to buy books that would help me better understand spirituality. I wanted to "get a handle" on where I was, how I could learn and grow. I discovered a whole new world. I tasted life and truth. It was as if I put on a new pair of eyeglasses and, for the first time, began to see what has always been. I wanted to learn, to see, and to grow into this new world. I no longer waited until the last minute to come to a prayer meeting or arrive just before it started. I was among friends. I actually started to believe that even God thought I was quite okay.

For the first time I went to a store that sold religious books. Over a period of time, I bought some Christian music albums and several books. Among these books were: *A Stranger to Self-Hatred: A Glimpse of Jesus* by Brennan Manning; *If You Really Knew Me Would You Still Like ME* by Eugene Kennedy; *Lord, Change Me!* by Evelyn Christenson; and *Why Am I Afraid to Tell You Who I Am?* by John Powell, S.J. Just reading these titles gives you a clear indication of where I was in my spiritual journey.

I knew there was a deeper level of life beyond what I had been living for roughly twenty-five years. I wanted to break away from my old ways, my old way of thinking and seeing, and be free. I wanted to change but I did not even know who I really was. Professionally, life could not have been better. I was secure in my accounting job. But now it was time to take care of myself personally and, for the first time, spiritually.

CHAPTER 5

God Loves Us So We Can Change

I knew something happened within me that night through the reading and teaching of that Scripture passage from Romans. I wanted this new awakening to continue even though it was impossible to predict where this would lead me. I was on some kind of journey, some kind of quest. I wanted more. I did not know what I had to do, but something had to give. This spark of new life was like a trickle of water, or a flicker of a flame; and now I wanted Niagara Falls, or an inferno. I did not know what to do, so I bought books on spirituality. Even though the books I was reading were written in the late 1960s and in the 1970s, their wisdom was timeless. I identified with each of them.

Through this reading, I was finally able to recognize and then put a name to what it was that had so much power and control over my life. It was FEAR. Whenever someone invited me to do something that seemed beyond my capability or comfort zone, I almost always said to myself, "But that's not me. You must have me confused with someone else."

This response or perception of myself limited my growth and the working of the Spirit of God. As Eugene Kennedy wrote:

We are often very successful in hiding what is best about us: our talents and strengths, the things that make us special human beings. We get so good at it at times that, despite all our brave talk about marching to different drummers, we blend ourselves completely into the blur of the crowd. We obscure what makes us unique and leave potential largely unrecognized and untapped. When we get good at it, we can even hide what we can be from ourselves … Better to hide who we are, we feel, than have ourselves exposed to ridicule, bland indifference, or outright rejection. (20-21)

I did not want to admit it, but FEAR had a powerful influence and stronghold over me. I was handcuffed by fear. As a student in high school, I avoided giving a speech or any oral presentation in front of a classroom. If the teacher gave the class the option to give a presentation or write a research paper, I always chose to write the paper. Even if I struggled to write a seven to ten page paper, it was better than having to speak in front of a class.

Little did I know that eventually the biggest challenge awaited me when I felt "called by God" to leave my accounting job, to join a Franciscan community, and pursue ministry and priesthood. I remember saying aloud to God, "God, you must have me confused with someone else." The negative messages that we give ourselves really stick and have great power over us. I believe God has been, and still is, breaking down those long-playing messages slowly but steadily. God has been so very patient with me, and at the same time, relentless. Thank God! Thank God that He did not give up on me, even when I wanted to give up on myself.

I purchased spiritual reading books to help me to change, and to understand what was happening within me.

I "digested" these books. After reading them, I decided: what I wanted to be like, what I needed to change, what I needed to get rid of, and what I could add to my personality. I wanted to be more visible, more open with others, and more likeable. I was on a mission to change myself. During this self-proclaimed mission, a unique thought, seemingly from nowhere, kept repeating itself in my mind: *turn yourself inside out.* I did not understand what this phrase meant. I found myself praying, "Lord, help me turn myself inside out".

One evening, while visiting with friends from the prayer group, someone suggested we break into small groups of three and pray for each other, taking turns with two praying for the one. This sounded like a good idea; after all, who would turn down prayer? It was my turn. A young man and woman prayed for me and with me.

The young man said after a period of time, "The Lord wants you to know this: Be gentle with yourself. Be gentle with yourself as I the Lord am gentle with you. I am not a rough God; I am a gentle God. Be gentle with yourself as I am gentle." It felt like someone had removed two thousand pounds off my shoulders.

After his prayer for me, the young woman, with much compassion and care prayed for me aloud: "Lord, help Bob turn himself inside out." I could not believe what I heard! I was stunned! That was my prayer, my idea. How did she know I was praying this? What I had thought was my prayer was actually God's prayer within me, God's desire for me. The Spirit placed that prayer within me.

The evening grew late, and it was time to leave. I walked the young woman to her car, and I asked her about the prayer she had spoken, about turning myself inside out. I asked if she had ever heard of this expression or prayed those words before. She told me, "No, it just seemed to be what I needed to say and pray for you." At that moment I knew it was the Spirit of God at work changing me from the inside out. I had become frustrated and exhausted by my lack of success to change myself. I needed to read once again the title of the book by Evelyn Christenson, *Lord Change Me!,* and remind myself it is God who changes us.

It had been my understanding when I was a young boy that God will love us *if* and *when* we change, because then God would see us as a little more loveable and a little more acceptable. In contrast, I was beginning to understand that Jesus' message was, "I will love you *so you can change."*

CHAPTER 6

Thanks for the Memories?

When I look at the cloud of fear that controlled me, I have to admit that what I was ultimately afraid of was rejection. Fear of rejection seriously affected me and influenced my way of thinking and behavior. Fear of all kinds is a major stumbling block for many if not all people, though most would not admit this. There is a Scripture passage that addresses our fears: "There is no fear in love, but perfect love casts out fear" (1 John 4:18). Apparently, it was time to address this fear in my life and to experience God's healing.

After I was involved with the Charismatic Renewal for about two years, I was on retreat for a weekend with some of my family at a Franciscan retreat house in central Wisconsin. The retreat began on a Friday evening and concluded after lunch on Sunday. Saturday afternoon, in the quiet of my room, I unexpectedly recalled a very painful and traumatic memory. Before I describe this memory, however, some background information is necessary.

I grew up shy and quiet, as I have already said. My first six years of grade school took place in a one-room schoolhouse. A small school was perfect for my type of personality. I had no idea what awaited me when I began my freshman year in high school. Already during the initial days of my freshman year, some senior boys and girls caught on to my shy ways. I was very naïve and easily intimidated. Why, I do not know; I just was.

There were four or five seniors who teased me, at first privately and discreetly. But as the year continued, they were less private and began to publicly embarrass and humiliate me. I did not know what to do or to say. Who could I tell? After all, I thought as a young adult male I should be able to handle this on my own. I felt totally alone, "exposed" and humiliated with nowhere to hide. I tried to avoid them in study hall, in the hallways, in the library, everywhere in school. Even when I was with my friends, they would not ease up.

Besides the public embarrassment, my physical health was affected as well. These seniors thought it was all in fun. I am sure they did not realize how humiliating and traumatic this was for me, and even if they did, they probably would not have stopped. In contemporary language, we call them bullies.

It was a happy, happy day when that senior class graduated from high school. Finally I was free, the bullying was in the past, and that is where the memories of the bullying belonged, or so I thought.

Meanwhile, back at the retreat, the Saturday afternoon conference ended, and we were invited to enjoy a reflective, restful and quiet remainder of the afternoon. I was sitting quietly and relaxing in my room. I suppose my eyes were closed, I cannot remember. To my complete surprise, what happened about eleven years prior, when I was a thirteen-year-old freshman in high school, came back vividly into my memory.

Something like a slideshow, like a video, appeared before me. I know it was not a dream. In this slideshow, I was again a freshman in high school. I stood by my locker along the wall in the hall of my school and turned the combination to open my locker. I turned to the final number of my combination and I slowly opened the door of my locker. Suddenly, those seniors came and slammed the locker door shut. The slamming of the locker door echoed throughout the hall. They laughed, and I stood there ashamed, embarrassed, and humiliated. Some of my classmates walked by and saw everything. I just died inside. Everybody knew! There was nowhere to hide. The painful emotions and humiliation were just as real as the day it happened eleven years ago. I thought all this was over, and I wanted it to stay in the past. Instead, through this memory, I stood at my locker reliving every bit of the pain of my freshman year.

Then this slideshow, this memory, moved in a surprising direction and in a way I will never forget. While I stood there feeling totally humiliated, Jesus stood to the left of the locker. I knew I was in the presence of love, unlike anything I had humanly experienced or known. I said to Jesus, "They are rejecting me!" His response changed everything. He said, "But I have never rejected you." Peace flooded over me, into every part of me. I had never felt this depth of peace. Everything changed. I changed! I cannot explain exactly what happened through this experience, but I know it was real. I did not think anything like this was possible, least of all possible for me.

Rejection, or what we perceive as rejection, is devastating. Rejection can be incredibly damaging and often has long lasting effects on people. Though an experience of rejection may have happened long ago, we still carry it with us daily whether or not we are consciously aware of it. It blocks our growth as human beings and makes us feel so alone. We fear that if it happened once, it can happen again.

I had heard and read about the "healing of memories" through the Holy Spirit, but paid very little attention to it. I know I did not make this memory and healing happen. This happened to me through the grace of God. All I can do is be grateful, extremely grateful. I never imagined that God was this <u>personal</u>, that I (we) matter this much to God and that God even knows what hurts us. I learned that what blocks our growth as a human being blocks our spiritual growth as well, and vice versa. Our growth as human beings and our spiritual growth cannot be separated. Being human and being "spiritual" have to happen together.

I know this healing was authentic and real, and truly the work of the Spirit. Some weeks after my retreat, I attended a conference and listened to a presentation on healing. After his presentation, the presenter invited anyone to come and share an experience of God's healing. I felt my heart racing, my hands sweaty. Though I loathed and avoided public speaking like the plague, I felt compelled to go to the microphone, and I did! I shared the story of my traumatic freshman year and the experience of healing. I told a crowd of about two hundred fifty people what I was once too embarrassed and ashamed to tell family or friends.

After I told my story, a considerable number of people came to talk to me. So many identified with my story. Some described their own painful memories when they were bullied, put down, or humiliated. Others found peace in the truth that God has never rejected them. People of all ages told me their stories and some told their own story for the first time. Whenever I tell my story of reliving the memory and the subsequent healing, the results are the same. People identify with it, and some feel peace for the first time.

As I look back at this healing of memories, I can see how important a relationship, an ongoing relationship, with our God is. Without a sense of God's presence, reliving those memories and feeling the pain would have been too much to bear. There would have been no healing, and I would have been left with only those same painful memories. But, with the Lord's presence, remembering and reliving those painful memories could not destroy me.

I also noticed I had no animosity toward those seniors in high school. In a rather strange way, I was even grateful for my freshman year because, through it, I came to know that God is so personal, and I came to know God's healing and acceptance, His non-rejecting presence. There is no rejection on God's side of our relationship. If there is rejection, it is from our side. Jesus said to the crowd, "Everyone whom the Father gives me will come to me, and I will not reject anyone who comes to me" (John 6:37).

CHAPTER 7

Learning My Religion

Because I attended public schools through the twelfth grade, I attended catechism classes my entire grade school and high school years. I went to catechism class first through eighth grade on Saturday mornings and high school catechism on Monday nights. Using the Baltimore Catechism with its question and answer format was perfectly suited for me. I memorized my lessons very well.

My sister and I practiced and practiced. She asked me the questions and I responded with the answers, word for word. I learned my religion well. My sister asked me, "Who made you?" I responded, "God made me." She continued, "Why did God make you?" My response was perfect, "God made me to know, love and serve Him in this world, and to be happy with Him forever in the next."

I was a model student of the Baltimore Catechism. I received high marks and numerous gold and silver stars. I felt good about my grades. My parents and teachers were proud of me. I really knew my religion, and I had the gold and silver stars to prove it. But sad to say, what I learned and memorized had very little personal impact or relevance.

The Baltimore Catechism provided words, words to explain what I supposedly believed and needed to learn.

Catechism classes did provide a good foundation to learn about the church and my faith. However, all that education through my twelve years of catechism did not address my image of God. All those years of catechism did not seem to draw me closer to God or God closer to me. When it came to God and love, it was one way: you must love God. My faith was not personal and had a very minimal impact on my life. I thought the gold and silver stars that my teachers awarded to me were good enough, but something was missing.

I knew we were commanded to love God, but how? How could I love God when I really did not consider God that loving or lovable? I questioned whether I was, in the eyes of God, lovable and worth loving. Most of my life, I pictured God shaking his finger at me, and watching for any misstep I might make. Where was I to turn? I began to read *A Stranger to Self-Hatred: A Glimpse of Jesus* by B. Manning after my experience with the passage from Romans. The author brought to light how our images of God have a powerful and far-reaching effect on our lives in positive or negative ways, whether we are consciously aware of it or not. I had so much to learn and so much to "un-learn."

I was so eager and energized to continue this quest, this journey to discover what seemed to me to be a new image of God. I really believe that somehow God was moving me, pushing me, pulling me forward. It felt like Jesus stood and knocked on the door of my life, of my heart, inviting me to open the door (Rev. 3:20). Unfortunately, I had kept that door securely closed. For years I identified with the following statement by J. Powell in his book, *Why Am I Afraid to Tell You Who I Am?*: "I am afraid to tell you who I am, because, if I tell you who I am, you may not like who I am, and if you don't like who I am, it's all that I've got" (12). I could not risk that.

Somewhat ironically, the basic principles of accounting symbolized my spirituality and spiritual life. In accounting, the goal is to have more assets than liabilities, more income than expenses. I lived my spiritual life in a similar manner. If I did more good and less bad, I was successful. I could feel good about myself and hopefully God felt good about me. I focused more on minimizing the liabilities than on maximizing the assets.

I thought that if I just avoided disobeying the commandments then God would approve of me and I would avoid any kind of punishment from God. What a terrible way to live! My spirituality was solely based on reward and punishment. Besides that, I did not think I was worthy of any kind of reward. But I definitely wanted to keep the punishment, or worse yet, God's disapproval, to a minimum. Unfortunately, I thought everything depended on me. Though I heard and learned about God's grace and unconditional love, I never thought it applied to me. My relationship with God was definitely a one-way relationship with everything depending on how I behaved or misbehaved.

Saint Teresa of Avila, the 16th century Spanish mystic, saw in a vision an angel rushing towards her, carrying a burning torch and a bucket of water. "Where are you going with that torch and bucket?" she asked. "What will you do with them?" The angel answered, "With the water I will put out the fires of hell, and with the fire I will burn down the mansions of heaven; then we will see who really loves God." How we image God shapes not only what we think God is like, but also what we think the Christian life is all about (Borg, 58).

Can we love God without the promise or hope of reward, or without the fear of punishment? In many ways our religion has been reduced to gaining a reward or avoiding punishment. For some, the purpose of religion is to avoid hell and get to heaven. Therefore, God is all about requirements, and Christianity is simply a means to satisfy those requirements now, for the sake of an eternal reward later. In contrast, the vision by St. Teresa of Avila speaks strongly that our life with God, our relationship with God, is about now, the present, and doing good for the sake of doing good in <u>response</u> to our relationship with God.

I now know why Christianity for me seemed like an uphill battle. I was initially trying to live my religion without a relationship with God. When we believe God loves us *if* and *when* we change, we are stuck. Nothing changes! Everything depends on us! We are continually stuck with unanswerable questions addressed to God such as: "God, *how much* do I need to change before you will love me and accept me? God, *what* do I need to change? God, when have I *changed enough* to satisfy you? *How* must I change to be more unlike myself so that you will consider me lovable, acceptable and worthy of your forgiveness?"

In the Scripture passage from Luke 7:36-50, a woman of "ill-repute" enters the house of Simon, the Pharisee. Jesus is there, too. The woman goes to Jesus, not to Simon. Simon greets the woman with looks of judgment, scowls, and condemnation. He stays comfortably at a distance, justifies his judgment, and is not at all affected by the woman. Because all Simon does is judge her, all the woman is able to see is her own sin. Both the woman and Simon, the Pharisee, are stuck and nothing changes.

The woman comes to Jesus and He does not turn her away, nor does He turn away from her. She feels accepted, welcomed, received, and not judged. In response, she lavishly and tearfully expresses her love for Jesus. She has encountered a love, an acceptance, a heart bigger than her own which could accept her when she could not accept herself; she experienced a heart bigger than her own which could forgive her when she could not forgive herself. This encounter, this experience, brought her to tears. When we take Jesus' message and His welcoming embrace to heart, we, too, might be brought to tears.

It has taken me many years to see, in a much different light, the commandment that Jesus calls the greatest commandment, "You shall love the Lord your God with all your heart, soul, mind and strength" (Mark 12:30). Does God need our love? Is God dependent on our love? Or rather, is it that we need to love God? Not just because it is a commandment, but when we love God, we discover and awaken to the truth that *it is God who loved us first*. First we are commanded to *love* God; then, hopefully, we *fall in love* with God; and finally, we *fall into* the love of God.

  To love God is a response to the love that is already ours. Indeed, in this light, our life is a response, a response not to *earn* God's love, but to *return* God's love. In effect, God says to you, to me and all creation, "I love you; love me back. Love me back by loving your brothers and sisters."

CHAPTER 8

Beauty in the Eyes of the Beholder

One summer, about four years after I joined the Franciscans, I helped at a retreat house in Wisconsin. I was one of the retreat directors for a week of private, guided retreats for religious sisters. Part of my role was to meet with the same three sisters individually each day for six days. Two of the sisters were quite easy to talk with and to direct. The other sister was a challenge. She was friendly and I could tell she was well intentioned. She had a sweet personality, but I could tell she was hurting and very sad. In our first meeting together, she told me about some recent events in her life, and she cried and cried. She talked about how poorly she was treated, not respected or appreciated, often put down, and even publicly humiliated.

I hoped our second meeting would be different, but there was no change. In the evening, all the directors at the retreat house who also met daily with sisters came together to evaluate the retreat thus far. Without violating confidentiality, I told my co-directors about this sister who was extremely sad, sad to the point of crying, almost uncontrollably. I did not know what to do, but I did know that the Lord did not want her to continue this way or to leave this week of retreat feeling this heaviness and sadness.

One of the directors suggested that I pick some flowers for her before our next meeting in the morning and give them to her. I did not see how this would help, but I was desperate to try anything to help her. Before I went to bed, a very strange idea popped into my mind and it would not leave. The idea came "out of the blue" to present her with flowers that matched the color of her dress. This did not make any sense to me. So far this week, she had worn very plain, one-color dresses. Her dresses were either light blue or light brown, and certainly not colorful. I turned off the light and went to sleep.

Early the next morning I went into our chapel for prayer with all the sisters on retreat and with the directors. I sat waiting for our prayer time to begin. As the chapel slowly filled, the sister with whom I was meeting walked in. She wore a wild, multi-colored, brilliant floral print dress. The dress looked so out of character for her. My eyes about popped out of their sockets. I knew I had my work cut out for me since I had planned to pick flowers that matched the colors of her dress. "What is going on?" I wondered.

After prayer I skipped breakfast and rushed outside to our beautiful grounds blanketed with flowerbeds. I hurriedly picked flowers of all colors. I did not have much time before our appointment. I found a vase in the retreat house, added some water, put the flowers in the vase, and put the flowers on a small table between my chair and hers. I hardly had enough time to sit down and catch my breath before she arrived.

Sister walked into our little meeting area wearing her wild floral print dress; she noticed the flowers immediately. Her eyes were glued to that floral arrangement like steel to a magnet. She could not take her eyes off the flowers. "They are so alive and beautiful!" she said excitedly. I responded, "I picked them for you. They are God's gift to you today." She said again with a smile, "They are beautiful!" I told her, "Take the flowers with you. We can meet again tomorrow morning." I felt like I was a small part of something much bigger happening. What was God doing? I had no idea what to expect next.

The next morning it was time for us to meet again. She walked into our meeting area with a beautiful, radiant smile. SHE was radiant. She told me she took the flowers to her room, and she was drawn into their beauty. She continued with a voice so peaceful and yet with a tone of excitement and surprise, "After a while, I walked outside. I noticed how beautiful everything was. The sky was so blue, the grass so green, the breeze so refreshing. I fell in love with nature. I looked around to check if anyone was looking, and I hugged a tree."

She could not take in all the natural beauty she saw and experienced. She talked as if she was in love, in love with nature, with God, and even with herself. We are like those flowers, we have a beauty within and, over time, the petals open to reveal the flower's inner beauty.

Beauty is so much a part of nature, and beauty is a part of who we are, of our very nature. We each have a part to play to bring our own created beauty into being. This created beauty resides within. God has placed it within us and it brings joy and beauty to our soul. It will move from the inside out transforming us into God's image and likeness. We reflect the beauty and splendor of the Father's love for us. Many people do not know, and therefore cannot see, their own goodness. They do not know or see their own God-given goodness and beauty.

Mary Beth Ingham, an author and professor, sheds some light on the connection between beauty and our spiritual life. Ingham asserts that the first step in any spiritual journey is to begin to see rightly, to notice what is present to us, to recognize the beauty around us. Once recognized, beauty leads the lover through the visible world to the spiritual realm, and to an awareness of God's presence within. From within this communion, the lover is transformed (12-13).

A classmate invited me to vacation with him in

California. We drove along the scenic coastline of the Pacific Ocean on the Pacific Coast Highway. We started at San Francisco and drove south. When we neared Monterey, we drove around a curve on the highway and a spectacular view of the coastline opened up for us. We had to stop. We stayed there a considerable amount of time trying to take in all the awesome beauty. No words were necessary between us. After some time, we got back into the car and continued our drive. I asked him, "I hope you do not mind that I asked you to stop. It was too beautiful to just keep driving." He replied, "No, I was hoping you would react that way." We had a wonderful time together taking our time and taking in the natural and gorgeous beauty of the California coastline.

When the school year began that following fall, I talked with one of my Scripture professors about my vacation in California and the drive on the Pacific Coast Highway. I told her about the beauty of the coastline and how we stopped so often. I took some pictures along the way, but the pictures could not adequately capture the magnificence of the scenery. My professor told me, "When you needed to stop and take in the beauty of the area, the beauty *within* you responded to the beauty outside of you. You were one with the beauty of your surroundings."

The God-given beauty within us reacts to the beauty of our creation, our created world outside of us. We are part of the created world, and the created world is a part of us. We are one with creation. I immediately think of St. Francis of Assisi and his love for nature and creation. St. Francis of Assisi is the patron saint of ecology. Because of his relationship with creation, he referred to nature in terms of Brother and Sister: Brother Sun, Sister Moon, Brother Air, Sister Water, etc.

A parishioner of a church at which I previously served, Cathy, wrote a letter to me that her mother had died. Sixteen days later, her father passed away from congestive heart failure and a broken heart after he lost his wife of sixty-six years. The parishioner wrote the following to me in her letter, "I must share a story with you about Mom the day before she died. She told me that she had seen God. I asked her what God looked like. She said, 'God has the beauty of every human being in Him.'"

The term "thin places" can be used as a metaphor to describe a time when we experience what we think is beyond ourselves. The term originated in Celtic Christianity and spirituality. Thin places are those places where the veil between this world and the next world is very thin. We can see what seemingly is beyond us, and yet it is not beyond us; it is right here.

Cathy's mother experienced that thin place where she could see God in a new and wonderful way. Her "seeing" shows us *there is something of us in God; there is something of God in us.* There is some beauty, some quality of God that we have in us that we are called to recognize, reflect and share. When God looks at us, God sees our own God-given and God-created beauty, even if we cannot see it ourselves. We each need to ask ourselves, "What is our God-created beauty that we reflect to others and reflect back to God? How is it that we cannot see this beauty within ourselves, and even worse, that we do not believe we even possess this type of beauty?"

The Scriptures are full of stories of God seeing in someone what they could not see in themselves. We are created in God's very image. When God looks at us, God sees a bit of Himself reflected right back! God looked at Sarah, a woman who saw herself as too old, and saw in her a mother of generations (Gn. 18: 9-19). God looked at Moses who saw himself as one who stutters, and God saw in Moses the freedom of the Israelites (Ex. 4: 10-12). While Samuel only could see in David a little boy, God saw in David a king like no other (1Sm. 16: 11-13).

While some might see in Mary only a young girl, God saw in her one who could carry the Christ-child (Lk. 1: 28-35). While the Pharisees saw only a blind man, Jesus saw the glory of God (Jn. 9: 1-41). While Jeremiah saw himself as only a young boy without much courage and ability to speak, God saw in him a courageous and great prophet (Jer. 1: 5-10). (bethquick.com: sermon 3-2-08, cycle A)

How does God see you? And how might that effect how you see yourself? If we could catch a glimpse of how God sees us and could see who we are in God, we just might be so overwhelmed that we would exclaim, "*God, you must have me confused with someone else!*" It could even bring us to tears.

CHAPTER 9

Turn Your Eyes upon Jesus; Look Full in His Wonderful Face

As an accountant, before I joined the Franciscan community, I worked in a public accounting firm. Beth, my co-worker in the computer department, was extremely efficient and dependable. She was about twenty-five years old. Beth had a bubbly personality, quick wit, and was enjoyable to work with and talk to. Professionally, Beth "had it together." However, her personal life was troubled and messy.

For some reason, Beth trusted me and told me about her personal life. She was not married although she was the mother of two absolutely beautiful children. Both the boy and the girl were pre-school age and had the same father. The father disappeared, wanting nothing to do with her or his children.

Even while raising these two children, Beth frequented the bars. At the end of the night she generally invited a guy to come to her apartment to stay overnight. She was very candid when she described her lifestyle. I told her over and over that she was much more than what she was doing. Unfortunately, she could not see her own value so she continued to follow this lifestyle, but something began to change in her.

During an income tax season, our business rented two satellite offices in addition to our main office to make it more convenient for our tax clients. One day I was away from the main office working at one of the satellite offices. During the afternoon I became distracted, or more accurately, pre-occupied.

For some unknown reason, I could not get the thought of Beth off my mind. I tried to ignore this pre-occupying thought, but I was not able to dismiss it. I decided that, if no other customers came to my office toward the end of my shift, I would return to the main office and talk with her. Maybe if we talked, this would relieve whatever thoughts were stirring in my mind.

By the time I returned to the main office after 5 pm., Beth had already left. I said to myself, "Oh well, that takes care of that. It is probably better that she is gone. Now I can let go of this heavy feeling when I think about her." I drove to my apartment, prepared a small supper, but I was not hungry. I lost my appetite. Those same thoughts about her returned, and I did not know what to do. I felt so restless. I turned on the TV, hoping I could get "back to normal." Finally, all I could do was give this to God. I did not know what else to do. All I could do was pray. So I took time away from the TV and my supper, and went in the other room to pray. I prayed as long as it took until I felt some peace from this heavy feeling and could finally let go of these thoughts and pre-occupation.

The next morning Beth came into my office. In a very troubled and quivering voice she said to me, "Last night I attempted suicide, but I failed." I felt a bit faint. She said she did not know what to do. She said sadly but with great conviction, "I don't want to live this way any more!" I did not know how to respond to her about anything she said. I sat there in shock and was speechless. I had no clear answers to anything. I was just glad that she was still with us.

A few days later something remarkable happened. I walked down the stairs that led to Beth's lower level office. She was sitting by her computer crying. I tried to turn around and leave before she saw me, but it was too late. She spotted me. I was stuck. I walked over to her and asked if she was all right. She continued to cry.

Beth reached down into her purse that was on the floor next to her chair. She pulled out a small card. While still sitting, she turned my way and held that card up close to my face. She asked me tearfully, "What do you see?" I responded, "It is a picture of Jesus." She asked again, emphatically, "No, No! What do you see?" I was at a loss for words. I asked her what she saw. With great passion and emotion, she said, "Look at his eyes! Don't you see his compassion?" Beth took the picture of Jesus and, looking at it, said, "I know now what I want. I want someone who wants me for who I am—not someone who wants me for what I can do for them." Beth repeated, "I want someone who wants me for who I am!"

© Concordia Publishing House

I couldn't believe what Beth was saying or how she spoke with such passion and longing. I was dumbfounded by this complete change in her. What happened to her? Beth had made a striking discovery. She had discovered her own God-given goodness, her true worth in the eyes of God, her own beauty! Shortly after that, Beth began to date a young man who had remained friends with her over the years. Over time he fell in love with those two wonderful children and with Beth, and they got married.

Before this life-changing event, I had never heard Beth say the word "compassion." Now, Beth was speaking so passionately about the compassion that she saw in Jesus' eyes. She absorbed it; she soaked it in. She was so hungry for it. In the book, *Jesus, the Way to Freedom*, the author, Donald Gray, writes:

> His [Jesus'] compassion enables us to be compassionate toward ourselves. It is the divine compassion that Jesus embodies in human history and in his own compassionate life and death. Before I am asked to show compassion toward my brothers and sisters in their suffering, I am asked to accept the Father's compassion in my own life, to be transformed by it, to become caring and compassionate toward myself in my own suffering and hurt, in my own failure and need. The Father's loving graciousness is not in any way conditioned by or dependent upon what we do. He will be gracious and compassionate toward us no matter what we are or do. (47)

"I can't live like this anymore! I can't go on like this!" Beth's cry for help, this brave and honest cry for help, probably saved her life. Maybe we all have, some time or another, felt like crying out, "I don't want to live like this anymore!"

There are too many who would rather be in a bad relationship, even a harmful or damaging relationship, than no relationship. Some people are caught up and controlled by their fears or anger. Some are entrapped by a poor image of themselves or a lack of self worth. Whatever the case may be, because some would rather be in a bad relationship than no relationship, they make one bad choice after another, and these choices cannot be free, loving, wise or life giving.

B. Manning writes about the importance of compassion:

> What would the Church be like if we erred from an excess of compassion rather than from a stingy and legalistic lack of it? … Jesus perceived that the only way people would experience life as gracious gift, the only way to help them to prize themselves as grace and treasure, was to treat them as treasure and be gracious to them. I can be anointed, prayed over, sermonized to, dialogued with and exposed to God's unconditional love in books, tracts, and tapes, but this marvelous revelation will fall on ears that do not hear and eyes that do not see, unless some other human beings refresh the weariness of my defeated days. Barring prevenient [meaning coming before] grace, I simply will not accept my life and being as God's gracious gift, unless someone values me, 'we can only sense ourselves and our world valued and cherished by God when we feel valued and cherished by others.' (32)

Clearly a predominant trait of Jesus is compassion. Jesus is the compassion of God. Jesus is the face of God. If we want to know what God is like, look at Jesus. God desires that everyone would personally know and experience His compassion. We are God's instruments. Let us show to others the face of God and be God's compassion for them.

CHAPTER 10

In Your Dreams

The year that I moved into my first Franciscan community was very challenging, mostly because of all the transitions that accompanied this change in my life. Before I moved into the community house, I had lived in an apartment, worked as an accountant, and owned a new car. Suddenly I was living in a religious community with about eighteen men from different areas of the country. I had grown up on a dairy farm, whereas most members of my community had been raised in large cities. When I enrolled in college as a freshman, I was twenty-nine years old. I took courses in philosophy and sociology, a gigantic change from my accounting past.

My early experience and initial attempt at ministry was not exactly a shining example of what ministry can be. I visited patients in a hospital on Sundays. I was very new at this. I was quite nervous as I walked into a hospital room to visit a patient. I covered up my nervousness by asking patients questions to avoid any awkward and silent moments. I peppered one poor man with questions. He appeared rather annoyed. He motioned for me to hand him the pad of paper and pen on the tray. I gave him the pad of paper and he wrote, "I cannot talk!" It was only then that I noticed the tracheotomy. I did not know what that was at the time.

I figured the surgery must have something to do with his inability to talk. I felt so embarrassed. To apologize to him, I grabbed the pad of paper and pen, and I wrote, "I'm sorry. I didn't know." Still annoyed, he took the pad of paper and pen from me and wrote, "I can't talk, but I can hear!"

Talk about feeling embarrassed. What a terrible beginning to ministry! I began to wonder if I was really cut out for this kind of work, this life of ministry. I was again asking myself, "Is this really for me?" I did not want to revert back to these same old thoughts and questions that had plagued me in the past, but here I was, again asking, "God, are you sure this is for me, or do you have me confused with someone else?" Fortunately, I hung in there despite my foibles, and I am glad I did.

However, these transitions to a new way of life, a life of ministry, took their toll on me, and my directors recognized this. They suggested that I meet with a counselor. I felt completely devastated by their suggestion. It was hard to hear and accept. I had never gone to a counselor, and I tried to convince myself that I didn't need counseling, that I was not "crazy." Little did I know going to counseling would be one of the best things I ever did.

After several sessions with my counselor and with some frustration, he declared, "We have hit a brick wall." I was stuck. He was stuck. Our counseling sessions were going nowhere. My counselor could not figure out what direction to pursue. Finally, he asked me, "Do you ever dream?" I told him. "If I did, I can't remember any." He explained, "Sometimes dreams can unlock, open up, and help us to see troublesome areas of our life that may block healing and growth. Dreams can help us to understand ourselves. Pay attention to any dreams in the next few nights and write them down."

I left that session more confused than ever. I called my ex-spiritual director and told her that my counselor suggested that I should keep track of my dreams and write them down. I was hoping my ex-spiritual director would say to me, "Now who is the crazy one!" But not only did she not respond that way, she replied with excitement, encouragement and strong conviction, "Oh, Bob dreams are a wonderful way for God's Spirit to speak to us. Dreams can help us to see and understand what is going on in our subconscious life. Dreams can be wonderful ways that lead to healing. I keep a dream journal myself." After our phone conversation, all I could do was give in and let it happen, and happen it did.

A few nights later, I had three consecutive dreams. I woke up and wrote in my dream journal as fast as I could what had happened in these three dreams, and more importantly, how I had felt at different moments during each dream. All three dreams involved my Dad and myself. It was apparent to me from these dreams that something had happened many years ago between my Dad and me that still had a lingering effect on my life.

In one of these three dreams, I was a very young boy on the farm. I heard someone say to me, "Hey, there are grapes growing in the garden!" I got excited and walked quickly to the garden. Sure enough, grapes were growing in the garden! I got all excited. As I walked through the garden, I even spotted grapes somewhat concealed by leaves. I just remember being so excited.

Then the scene in my dream switched and my Dad was sitting on the porch by the house. I slowly came out of the house and noticed him sitting on the chair. I walked over to him, carrying my vines loaded with grapes from the garden. I said to my Dad, "Did you see the grapes growing in the garden?" He took some, tasted the grapes, and enjoyed them. I handed all my grapes to him, and I walked away empty-handed and feeling sad.

I returned to my counselor the next week. From my dream journal, I read to him my three dreams. After I read the first dream, he told me that there are some really good things happening, as well as sad things. First, the good. The garden is a place of growth. The garden is a place where new life happens and grows. The garden is you. Grapes are a symbol of joy and life. You are excited about this new life growing in you. You even notice the grapes that are somewhat concealed and only partially visible. Though concealed, you know there is growth and life there.

Then my counselor told me the not so good. You see your Dad and you are all excited to tell him about this new growth that has taken root inside of you. You offer him some grapes so he can see and taste it for himself. But either you give it all to him or he takes it all. In the end, you walk away empty, and can no longer feel excited about this new life and growth inside of you.

After these counseling sessions, the months that followed were not only tough for me emotionally, but they were also physically draining. I became preoccupied with what was surfacing and stirring inside of me because of these dreams. At times, I even had difficulty maintaining a normal conversation. I could not concentrate on my studies, and my grades were slipping. I could not keep any kind of focus. I wanted to get rid of all these feelings. I wanted to be alone and to isolate myself.

Then one evening a fellow Franciscan came to our community house to join us for a meal. After the meal, he came to me and asked how I was doing. I immediately told him, "I'm doing well." I was lying, of course. I had hoped to convince him that everything was all right. He came right back with, "No, no you're not." Surprised by this, I replied, "What? What do you mean?" He said, "No you're not. I would not be praying for you like I have been if you were doing all right."

He continued, "For some reason, God has been leading me to pray for you. Now, tell me, what is going on?" We broke away from the rest of the community and talked for a long time. Because he felt so strongly called to pray for me, this helped me to believe that God was with me in this mess. I could trust God and trust that I was not alone. I now believed that something good would come from these dreams and from what stirred inside of me, though I did not know how this would finally unfold. God knew what was best for me. All I could do was trust and believe that God would work this out. God had to do for me what I could not do for myself. However, I did not have a clue what that might be.

Several weeks passed. Then an opportunity came for me to attend a weekend retreat. The retreat began on a Friday night. The retreat leader talked about the relationship between Jesus and the Father, about the Father's relationship with the Son, and the Son's relationship with the Father. As I listened, I became emotional but did not know why. I knew it had something to do with the Son's relationship with the Father. My dreams were about my relationship with my Dad, my biological father.

On Saturday afternoon I was alone in my room, and a boyhood memory flashed in my mind. I was probably three or four years old. I was sitting by the dining room table with my Mother and Dad and we were eating. My mother said that I should try some particular type of food she made. I told her that I didn't want to. But she insisted, "Just try a little." I didn't want to. Finally after several attempts to get me to try it, she spooned out some onto my plate. I said, "I didn't want it, and now it has touched the other food on my plate." I was a fussy eater at that age, and I did not like the different foods on my plate to touch. I just sat there and refused to eat. In disgust my Dad said, "If you do not want to eat, get away from the table!"

I ran from the table into the bedroom and slammed the door behind me. In my memory, I could tell how hard I slammed the door. The pictures hanging on the wall jiggled a little. I flopped on the bed and cried. My mother came to the door and said to me from behind the closed door, "Dad didn't mean it. Come on back to the table." I didn't know what to do.

Back in the present, reacting to these memories still so vivid in my mind, I silently cried out, "I don't know what to do!" I felt so alone with no one to turn to. "How can I go back to the table? What will they think of me?" But then, I felt God so present, so near, and God spoke tenderly to my heart, "I have never rejected you! I have never turned away from you!"

With those words, everything suddenly changed. Total peace came over me and through me. Everything was okay. At that moment, I quietly but resolutely said, "Today I claim you as my Father." I realize that "Father" is a word that for some attracts and for others causes fear or even fright. I now felt safe to be a son of the Father of Jesus.

I knew from that time on that I was and am a son of my Father. I have an earthly father. But I also have a "Heavenly" Father as well. It was like I said to God, "I will be son to you" and God replied, "I will be Father to you."

After this event, this memory flashback, I felt filled with so much peace. I felt such joy, such deep-down peace that settled everything inside of me. I was even grateful for the whole mess I went through: how I had felt when they recommended counseling; the counseling sessions themselves; the three confusing but revealing dreams; and how I had been so preoccupied, distracted, and troubled by these dreams. I thanked God for the healing and truth that came from those memories and the healing of my relationship with my Dad.

I learned through these dreams that it is crucial to focus on *how we interpret* life events. I was just a child. A child left alone after some scolding or punishment will interpret an event as a child. In my interpretation as a child, I felt that I not only disappointed my Dad, but that *I was a disappointment* to my Dad. I unknowingly or subconsciously assumed, therefore, that I must be a disappointment to God as well. At times we naturally and unknowingly project onto God the ways we interpret our experiences.

One of my spiritual directors helped me understand

more fully what God was doing through these dreams, the retreat, and the healing of my relationship with my Dad. She said that the most important healing we can experience involves our parents or other authority figures.   These healings automatically and directly affect how we "see" God, and how we interpret our relationship with God who is, for most of us, our greatest authority figure.

CHAPTER 11

Adam and Eve and the Fall; but How Far Can We Fall?

Most of my life I wanted to blame Adam and Eve. I felt that it is because of them that we all start out bad. It is because of Adam and Eve that we have to work so hard to get back into God's good grace and favor. It is because of them that we have to deal with sin and death. This just is not fair! Adam and Eve ate the apple and all of us are stuck paying for it! If only they would have obeyed and not eaten from that tree. It is their fault that we are in this mess!

I wanted to blame Adam and Eve as if their story were real, as if it really historically happened exactly this way. While it is a real story, this does not mean it actually and exactly happened as written. In other words, this story can be profoundly true even though not literally factual or an actual event.

When people ask, "Is that story true?" they usually mean, "Did it happen?" Stories can be true, that is, they can reveal truth even if they are not factual. In other words, we can say, "I do not know if it happened this way or not, but I know this story is true." These kinds of stories invite us into a particular way of seeing. These stories invite us to see both reality and our lives in a different, more insightful way (Borg, 50-52).

After Adam and Eve ate of the forbidden tree, God searched for Adam. God called out, "Adam, where are you?" Some conclude that God was very angry, searching out, ready to punish and shame Adam and Eve. Crouched among the trees, Adam and Eve hid from God because they did not want God to see them.

God called out to them, "Where are you?" By God asking Adam where he was, God was not asking Adam to name a place, some spot or geographical location in the garden. Instead, God was asking Adam about his state of mind. God asked, "Adam, what has happened to you? Why have you fallen into this condition of being afraid of me?" Adam closed his ears to the voice of the One who made him, the One who knew him completely, the One whose breath brought life into him (Reiser, 16).

Why do we think we must make every effort to escape the presence of God, the gaze of God? What are we afraid of? I was taught, and always thought, that the "great fall in the garden" was Adam and Eve's sin, their disobedience. Was their sin the great fall, or did the real fall, the disastrous fall happen *after* their sin? In other words, did the great fall actually happen when they became afraid of God and, in their fear and shame, hid from God? Which might be more "deadly," the sin we commit, or falling into hiding, into a hidden life that causes so many problems? How have we *fallen* into this way of living? The degree to which we as persons hide from God determines how far we can fall.

The author, W. Reiser, S. J. continues:

Being uncovered and totally open to God's view is the state God intended for us; it is the basic condition of our creaturehood. Why do we think we must try to hide our real

condition from God, or from one another,
or even from our own selves? Perhaps this
strange need to hide lies at the root of most
human sin. And even if we had a reason,
where on earth could we flee to avoid the
divine presence? What is there about us that
God does not already know? (17)

Some years ago, I served as a chaplain in a prison.
During my chaplaincy, I met an inmate who I will remember
forever. I entered his cell and introduced myself. I will say
his name was Bill (not his real name). We talked briefly.
He did most of the talking, and that was fine with me. Bill
asked me a most unexpected question, "Rev, what is your
favorite Scripture?" I certainly did not expect our visit and
conversation to take this direction.

He pulled his Bible off his shelf, and then a second
Bible, and gave it to me. Then he said, "I'll show you my
favorite Scripture and you show me yours." I said, "That
sounds like a good deal." Embarrassingly, I could not find
mine. I could not remember where in the Bible the Scripture
was located. Bill opened his Bible and found his favorite
passage immediately. He showed me Rom. 3:23. He began
to read, "All have sinned and fallen short of the glory of
God." I could not believe what I was hearing! This was
the Scripture I had been trying to find. I said with great
disbelief, "Bill, that's the passage I was trying to find." I
thought to myself, "I don't believe this! Coincidence? What
are the chances? How could this happen? God, what do
you want to do here?"

Bill showed me the passage in his Bible. He had
highlighted verse three, "All have sinned and fallen short of
the glory of God." Feeling confused, I asked him, "Bill, you
have not highlighted the rest of the passage. You missed
the best part! You are missing the good news!" I continued
to read to him the very next verse, Rom. 3-24, "But all are
justified by the free gift of God's grace through being set free

in Christ Jesus."

He looked at me and, although we made eye-to-eye contact, it was more accurately a heart-to-heart contact. Bill said sadly, "I didn't highlight the rest of the passage because I don't believe it." I took his Bible from him and quickly paged through it. I noticed how many passages he had highlighted. But, without exception, he consistently only highlighted the passages with negative connotations. I felt so sorry for him because he did not know what he was missing. For example, in the Gospel of Luke, 21:17, "All will hate you because of me." Bill only highlighted the words, "All will hate you."

I was filled with sadness for Bill and felt helpless. I could not get Bill to see, to believe the Good News. He could not believe the Good News, the Good News of God's grace. Yes, Bill had sinned. There was no doubt that Bill had sinned. But, we all have sinned and we all have fallen short of the glory of God. Yes, Bill had fallen. But the real question became, how far would he fall? Bill had such a negative image of God and himself that he could not stop his fall.

Bill described his awful childhood. Through his growing up years, he had felt unwanted, unloved, abandoned, rejected, and invisible to his family, especially his parents. He made a bad choice later on in life; he committed a crime and he will be confined the remainder of his life, isolated from society forever.

I will always remember my visit with Bill, especially the moment when our eyes met, but more accurately, when our hearts met. All I could see and feel was his deep emptiness and how far he had truly fallen. I felt totally helpless. Nothing I could say would convince him of his own worth or reverse the downward spiral he had accepted as his fate. He had sunk and fallen so deeply into his own unworthiness and despair; he could not see any way out. He lived in two prisons, the actual prison building and his own inner prison.

CHAPTER 12

MERCY Is His Name

My Franciscan community strongly recommends that we each make an annual retreat. I contacted The Dwelling Place in Mississippi and scheduled a one-week retreat in February of 2001. I cleared my calendar, escaped from my busy schedule and appointments, and entered into the silence and beauty of nature with no phones, television or newspapers. My time was my own except one hour each day when I met with my director.

With no distractions or commitments, I realized how tired I was. My director summed it up in one concise sentence: "Fatigue has a way of catching up with us when we have the time to be tired." Exactly! On the third morning of my retreat, I met with my director again. She suggested that, since I was finally rested, she would like me to do an exercise of the imagination. She said, "Sometimes the Spirit can work better when we 'get out of our heads', and then, through our imagination, we see things differently." She suggested the following: Imagine you are in some kind of enclosure. You are alone. You hear a knock on the door and it is Jesus. That is all she told me. I gave her a blank look because that is how I felt, totally blank. But I trusted that the Spirit of God was working through my director and her direction. We concluded our time together, and I went back to my hermitage.

Off and on, it seemed like hours, I struggled with how to jumpstart my imagination given her instruction and her brief scenario. I tried numerous times to put myself "into a state" where I could imagine something, anything. I wished she had given me more to go on, more to spark my imagination. But there I was. I could not make it happen. I tried everything I could. Nothing worked.

Finally, after trying and trying, I relaxed in my recliner, and without really trying any more, my imagination took over. This is what I "saw" in my mind's eye: I am in a rustic type shack/cabin in the woods. Everything in the cabin is made of wood. It is a sunny day and the sun is shining brightly through the trees. I am sitting on the side of my bed, resting, waiting, and ready for this moment. I hear a knock on the door and I spring from my bed and open the door. There He stands. Jesus looks a bit rustic Himself. He has a bit of a smile on His face though I do not notice any specific facial features. It does not matter. I just stand in the presence of total peace, warmth, love and acceptance. It seems as though all time is standing still.

His arm casually rests against the doorway and I just stand there. I do not know what to do. Should I shake His hand, give Him a hug? I am speechless. His look is so peaceful. He is so relaxed and He does not say anything. It seems no words are necessary, not even a greeting. It was as if we imagined this meeting would happen, and now it finally has and I just stand there. His presence melts me, warms me. All that matters is that He is here with me and I am here with Him. I do not know how long we stand there, speechless. All that matters is that this wonderful time is happening.

I seem to come to and realize that I have not asked Him in. Where were my manners? We both walk to a table inside the cabin and sit down. Then, like a rapid slideshow, my past years pass before me: my early years, my childhood, my youth, and my adult years. All the stuff, the memories, the things that I had done and the things that happened to me rapidly pass before my eyes. All the stuff I was not proud of, that I was even ashamed of, and that I had never told anyone, passed rapidly before me.

When the "slideshow" concluded, an amazing feeling came over me. All that stuff I had been holding against myself, I suddenly realize *He did not hold against me!* What incredible mercy! It did not hurt any more. We speak no words. No words are necessary. I realize it is all O.K! All I can do is cry with joy and extreme gratitude knowing that He has made it so. Imagine yourself, eye-to-eye with Jesus, knowing at that very moment He knows everything about you, and He says to you, "Neither do I condemn you." That is what it felt like.

Before this experience, I could never look back at my life without feeling some guilt, without feeling as if something had gone wrong, and I held all of that against myself. But now I realize that my past was all O.K. He just sat there and smiled at me, knowing what is happening. My past is all forgiven! It is all O.K!

The past events and the memory of those events are not erased. However, more importantly and more unbelievably, the guilt and shame I connected to my memory of those events no longer plagues me! The good, the bad, the ugly, all of it, all the past is O.K. It is better than O.K. It is all blessed with His presence. I could only sit and look at Him, and say, "You knew it all, all the time, you knew it all." He smiled at me. I said, "This is what you are all about! This is the great work you do!" I could not believe it. He took such pleasure from this moment. I could only sit and feel so very grateful.

I needed to mark this moment in time. I brought out some food. It was just some bread. I knew He liked bread. We sat and ate with still no conversation. All that mattered was that He was here with me and I was here with Him. It was quiet intimacy. We ate ever so slowly enjoying every bite, every moment. It seemed to last forever, but went by so fast, too fast.

After we broke the bread, Jesus began to draw me toward Himself, to His heart. I felt it. I felt Him say, "This is a new day, and this is a new time." I was now ready for a new call, a new kind of walk with Him. I felt stronger when He said this, stronger than I had ever felt. Suddenly, there was a seriousness in Him, an urgency in His voice and demeanor. I said, "I am ready" and He said, "No, we are ready." I looked at Him. I could only say "Yes," not verbally, but He knew it. I could only trust Him. It was a new day; it was a new time! What He did in my life was only getting me ready for what was ahead. How could I not trust Him? I wanted Him to stay, but I knew it was time for Him to go.

The next thing I knew, I was back sitting in my recliner at the retreat house. I have no clue how much time passed during this experience. I will never know. I asked myself, "What just happened?" I wrote everything down. I felt so grateful, so blessed. I looked at a book by William E. Reiser, S.J, *Drawn to the Divine: A Spirituality of Revelation.* I was attracted to the chapter entitled "The Religious Experience of Jesus' Disciples" in which he wrote what Jesus' disciples experienced and how their lives changed as they came to know and follow Him (Reiser, 67-103).

One experience of Jesus' disciples paralleled mine perfectly. Disciples understand themselves as loved sinners. Though Ps. 51:5 rightfully asserts, "My sin is always before me," still *at the same time* we are loved and accepted. There were events from my life in that slideshow that no one knew, but the Lord knew.

Jesus delighted to heal them, forgive them, without any kind of accusation, shame, blame, or punishment. I felt like a loved sinner. I was not *either* loved or a sinner, I was *both* loved and a sinner. I had thought these two words could not go together. Being a *loved sinner* sounds like two opposites; however, one does not cancel out the other. As a commentary, Reiser writes: "Because Jesus was trying to uncover for them the basic truth about us, [about everyone], that we are first and foremost children of God; we may be sinners, but we are deeply loved" (Reiser, 78-9).

I had never thought about my life with God in this way. It makes perfect sense. What else can we be but loved sinners? This is truth! One does not cancel out the other. We are called to live in the middle of this truth, this identity. We are sinners, but this does not cancel out God's love, God's incredible unconditional love, his gift of grace and presence. We are loved, but this does not cancel out the fact that we are sinners and that we are called to live responsible and accountable lives that are good. I recall the following statement that applies here: "God isn't upset with sinners; God is upset with those who don't think they are sinners."

When we live <u>in the middle</u> of this identity of being a loved sinner, we live in the truth of who we are. We can be honest with our own selves and God. When we live in the middle of this truth, prayer happens more naturally and genuinely. We are at peace. We are humble and thankful. Joy is even possible. We tend to act with more compassion and mercy because we have experienced the compassion and mercy of God. It is much more difficult to judge others because we know that we too have sinned, and that the other person is also a loved sinner.

Could this be what God's mercy, God's grace and goodness are like? Another way of saying this: "God, you have seen me at my best, you have seen me at my worst, and still you do not walk away. Still you love me. Still you accept me." We can only be extremely humble and grateful, when we live in this truth and identity of a loved sinner.

Who would have thought it would be our own sins, our own imperfections that would most often lead us to Jesus? How good it is, what Good News this is, that we never need to be afraid to acknowledge our sinfulness or our failings out of fear of being turned away. God is not going to leave us, though we may leave God.

It is time to come out of hiding. It is time to forgive,

especially to forgive ourselves, for God's name is MERCY. When we try to run away or hide from our true selves, we also run away or hide from God. When we try to hide or run away from God, we also hide or run away from our true selves. Running and hiding are so tiring, so exhausting. It wears us out and gets us nowhere. It is time to be honest with God and to be honest with our own selves. It is time for truth, the truth that will free us, the truth that we are loved sinners.

When we deny the truth that we are both loved and sinners at the same time, we get stuck. When we emphasize only the sinner part, we may fall into the trap of what I call the downward spiral. We cannot see our own goodness, we think we can never measure up or live up to what we think God expects of us, or what we expect of ourselves or think anyone else expects. We may become scrupulous and question all our actions, all our thoughts. There is no freedom, no cause for joy or gratitude. We are trapped inside ourselves.

On the other hand, we can also become stuck when we deny the sinner part of our identity as loved sinners. God is not upset with sinners; God is upset with those who do not think they are sinners. People who think of themselves as flawless must maintain a self-image of perfection. They feel that if someone were to come to know their imperfections or weaknesses, that would destroy them, and they cannot risk that. Therefore, in extreme cases, they must "destroy," discredit, or even demonize the character of others who know their imperfections before their own imperfections can be exposed.

In his very insightful book, "*People of the Lie*," M. Scott Peck writes:

> In their hearts, they consider themselves
> above reproach, so they must lash out at
> anyone who does reproach them. They
> sacrifice others to preserve their self-

image of perfection. … In other words, they attack others instead of facing their own failures. Spiritual growth requires the acknowledgement of one's own need to grow. … While they seem to lack any motivation to be good, they intensely desire to appear good. Their "goodness" is all on a level of pretense. It is, in effect, a lie. This is why they are "people of the lie." Actually the lie is designed not so much to deceive others as to deceive themselves. … the essential component of evil is not the absence of a sense of sin or imperfection, but the unwillingness to tolerate that sense. … We become evil by attempting to hide from ourselves. The wickedness … is committed … as a part of this cover-up process. Evil originates not in the absence of guilt, but in the effort to escape it. (73-76)

What we look for as human beings is someone who knows everything about us and still loves us all the way through, *all the way through* our fears, failures, self-doubts and self-inadequacies, where we think we are not enough, where we cannot love ourselves.

In the story of the Woman at the Well (Jn. 4: 1-42), a Samaritan woman comes to the well to get water. Jesus is there. Jesus is Jewish. In the opinion of the Jews, Samaritans are worthless. Besides that, she is a woman, and even in Jewish society, women at best, are treated as second-class citizens.

To the woman's surprise, Jesus does not treat her as she expected to be treated. He does not reject, judge or belittle her. After establishing some conversation and trust, Jesus brings up a subject that causes terrible shame and embarrassment for the woman, the subject of her husband. "Go and call your husband, Jesus says to her, and come back here!" The woman admits, "I have no husband." Jesus tells the woman that she is right in saying she has no husband; in fact, she has had five, and the one she is with is not her husband.

Still Jesus does not reject her, shame her, or berate her. Instead He loves her all the way through. In effect Jesus says to the woman, "Where you experience shame, I will love you there! I will heal you there! I will forgive you there! I will accept you there! I will pour out my mercy there! I will reveal myself there! I will *save you* there! That is what a Savior does!"

The woman is so moved and ecstatic that she forgets why she had come to the well. She leaves her water jar and hurries into town to tell the people that they must meet this man who knows everything about her, and still loves her there, still loves her all the way through. He has got to be the Savior of the world! After her encounter with Jesus, she knew herself as a loved sinner, and that truth and identity changed almost everything.

CHAPTER 13

Intimacy Goes Both Ways

One summer when I was in my mid-twenties, my brothers, sister, their spouses and I all came to the farm where my parents still lived. We planned a cookout complete with brats, a real Wisconsin favorite, and hamburgers on the grill. Eventually our conversation changed direction. We began to talk about church, faith, Scripture, Jesus, etc. During our conversation, I noticed Dad had become increasingly uncomfortable.

He tried to hide his reactions, but I could tell he was covering up. He walked away. I followed him. When I caught up with him, we talked. I told him that I could see he was uncomfortable with our conversation. He didn't say anything at first, but then he turned, looked me in the eyes, and said to me with an emotional quiver in his voice, "I don't know how you can say the name Jesus without breaking down. My main concern when I go to church is that I might become emotional and look foolish." Wow! I could not believe what I had just heard! I didn't know what to say. I hadn't realized that my Dad's love for the Lord was so strong, so deep, so personal, and so much a part of his life.

I could tell from his emotional response he was

caught up in this relationship, in the flow of giving and receiving love between himself and the Lord. It was a mutual, two-way relationship. I had been privileged to get a glimpse of this rich flow of life and love between my Dad and the Lord. In a way, he was *living inside* of another Life, this Life of intimacy between himself and the Lord. When this Life touched his own life, it brought him to tears.

As I was preaching a sermon one day, I found myself saying to the congregation that we are invited to *live our life from the Life that lives within us.* I had never used this expression before, and I actually surprised myself that I could string such a series of words together and have them make sense. I knew what I was saying, and I think some of the congregation understood as well.

It is this Life, this Life that is bigger than our own, more loving and more forgiving, that begins to change us from the inside out. God loves us so we can change, not when and if we change then God will love us. God cannot love you or me more than God is loving us at this very moment, at this very second. Can we receive and believe this truth? Can we live in this acceptance of being accepted? Can we trust this grace and acceptance? When it seems too good to be true, we probably are getting close to the truth of who God is for us, and to the God and Father whom Jesus revealed.

This life and love of God within us is the indwelling of the Holy Spirit. We have all been given a share of this Holy Spirit. The Holy Spirit is this *God-life* (noun) living within us. The work of the Spirit is an inward, interior, and invisible work that reveals itself though our outward actions and through how we relate with others and our world. Indeed the indwelling of the Spirit within us is a mutual indwelling, that is, God is living in us and we are living in God. This mutual indwelling of "lives" becomes so intertwined that lines become blurred. We do not know where one life ends and the other life begins.

This connection between God and ourselves can

become so strong, so packed with meaning, and can even be so life-changing that we may eventually be led to say, "God, let your life happen in me! God, let your love happen in me! In my hands, my feet, my voice, my listening, in the way I hear, in the way I see, in my mind, in the way I think, in the very way I live!"

God's own life rubs off on us and we are changed or transformed from the inside out. Where once we were impatient, now we discover newfound patience; something that once upset us does not seem to matter as much anymore. We find peace that we cannot explain. Something that we once thought we could not live without does not seem as important. We are being changed from the inside out.

God is loving in us and through us, God is forgiving in and through us, God is showing mercy and compassion in and through us. It is much more the *allowing* of this presence and indwelling of God-life to act in and through us. In this way we live our lives from the Life that lives within us, and we do not know where one life ends and the other begins. As St. Paul so beautifully discovered, "It is no longer I who live, but it is Christ who lives in me" (Gal. 2:20).

In the book *Lord, Change Me!*, Evelyn Christenson echoes our invitation to live our life from the Life that lives within us. Christenson writes, "In my Bible I wrote, 'Ego moves to the side—Christ moves to the center.' The how to change was becoming obvious. I was to let Christ live in me, transforming me into the likeness of Himself" (26).

I ate at very few restaurants when I was a young man. I did not eat many tossed salads. I did not like the salad dressings that most restaurants offered. Remember, I was a fussy eater. When they would serve me a tossed salad, there was either too little dressing on the salad leaving the tossed salad too dry, or the salad was saturated with dressing. While with a friend at a restaurant, he ordered a dinner and a salad came with his meal. He told the waitress he wanted French dressing and said, "I would like my dressing on the side." I did not know that I could have my tossed salad exactly the way I wanted. I could add as much or as little dressing. Not too much, not too little, but exactly how much I wanted.

We sometimes treat God in a similar manner. I have my life before me (salad). I have my dressing on the side (God). I pour just a little, but not too much God into my life. Not too much. Not too little. I add only as much as I want. Living this kind of spirituality, this kind of life with God, will get us nowhere. A statement that I often repeat over and over to myself and that has helped me to focus and be attentive to this mutual relationship, this mutual intimacy is simply saying, "I am here with You; You are here with me. All is well."

CHAPTER 14

Knowing That We Are Known

I try to be as faithful as possible about sending greeting cards to friends, relatives, family and special acquaintances on their birthdays and on holidays. Well, here it was, another Christmas and Holiday Season, and I needed to send a card to a dear and close friend. I bought a beautiful card and I really liked the message printed in the card. I sat at my desk, opened the card, and reread the message. I wrote her mailing address and my return address on the envelope. I licked a stamp and placed it securely in the upper right hand corner of the envelope. It was now time to write something personal in the card. This was the hardest part.

What should I write? This part is always the great challenge, is it not? I wrote, "It is so good to know you." I felt relatively pleased with that, and it certainly was true. But I needed to write more. She was and still is such a wonderful friend. I continued to write, "and to be known by you." Wow! Where did that come from? My own words took me by surprise. After I wrote those words, I discovered something wonderful about our friendship, and I discovered something wonderful about the nature of friendship and relationship itself.

I was especially pleased with that second part that I wrote. I sat back, looked again at what I had written, and thought, this is exactly what I want her to know. These words really described our friendship because it was so mutual. This is exactly what I wanted to say, what I wanted her to know, through this card. "Yes! It is so good to know you and to be known by you." I slipped the card into the envelope and took it to the mailbox.

A few days later, I received a phone call from my friend. She had received the Christmas card, and she thanked me. She commented on what I had written. She loved it! We talked about our friendship, our relationship that had formed, and the very nature of friendship. She wanted to talk about the last part I had written, "… it is so good to be known by you."

We talked for a while about what these words meant. Together we realized, this is it, is it not? This is what we as people, as human beings, really hunger for! This is what we long for through friendship, maybe even in life. It does not matter what age or stage of life we are in. How good it is to be known by another person, as we are, with all of our strengths and weaknesses, our good days and bad days, our "good stuff" and our flaws. How good it is to know another, but especially how good it is to be known by another, and to <u>know</u> it. In other words, *how good it is to know that you are known.*

In that knowing, we are invited by another to live in that incredible acceptance, friendship and love. How freeing that is! How life-giving, encouraging, energizing, self-assuring, and even healing! We want the best for one another, and want to draw the best out of each other.

If this is true with our human relationships, can it also be true with our relationship with God? Of course it is impossible to completely know God. I think we can all agree with that. Yet, in the Scriptures it is written, "Eternal life is this; to know you, the only true God and Jesus Christ whom you have sent" (John 17:3, NJB). The footnote in my Bible for this passage elaborates on the word "know." It reads as follows: "In Biblical language, 'knowledge' is not merely the conclusion of an intellectual process, but the fruit of an 'experience,' a personal contact and when it matures, it is love."

If knowing that we are known is a true quality and characteristic of a deep, mutual friendship, how does this apply to God and our relationship with God? Can I say, "God, it is so good to be known by you and to know that I am known by you?" IS THIS POSSIBLE? There is no end to the level or depth of relationship into which God invites us. God will take us deeper and deeper. God will take us as far as we are willing to go.

One evening when I was still involved with the Charismatic Renewal and before I joined the Franciscan Order, the leader of our prayer meeting talked about how God sees us. She said that God has a name for us, a name so personal that the name fits us perfectly. I listened to her teaching with some skepticism, I admit. After the meeting concluded, I drove back to my apartment. I said aloud to God in the car, "Ok, if this is so, if you have a name for me, I sure would like to know it."

I arrived at my apartment, put my key into the door lock, and opened the door into the front room. Instead of putting on the light, I walked over to the window overlooking the city. My upstairs apartment was high enough that I could get a good overview of the city. I stood there and looked out my window to see how beautiful the city looked at night under the glow of lights. I stood there for a long time.

I began to slowly realize I do this a lot, namely, I look out a window. I do this without being consciously aware of it. I thought maybe windows might have something to do with God's name or the teaching at the prayer meeting tonight. I quickly dismissed the thought; I could not do anything about it anyway and went to bed.

Early one morning in the same week, as I was getting

ready to go to work, I turned on my television. A Christian talk show was on. The guest gave a brief Bible teaching. One of his Bible passages came from Malachi 3. He invited the viewers to open their Bibles.

My Bible was nearby, so I opened it and read along, "See if I will not open the windows of heaven for you and pour down for you overflowing blessing" (Mal. 3:10). When I heard this, I got quiet. It seemed time stood still. In the middle of that passage appeared the word "window." Was this an odd or crazy coincidence? I never noticed this Scripture before. Is this connected with the night I stood at my window and looked out over the city? I somewhat dismissed this thought and left for work. I was probably making too much of this.

During the entire next prayer meeting, I could not get these thoughts about "window" out of my mind. I could not let it go, and I felt the need to talk with the leader when the meeting ended. I told her what had happened during the week after she said that God had a name for each of us. I told her about the events and significance of "window." She asked me if I was willing to pray about that right now. I had not expected her invitation to pray, but why not.

She prayed with me about these events, addressing God in such a beautiful, personal and loving way. She asked God to clarify what might be happening, and thanked God for all this and for me. I felt drawn into our prayer. During her prayer, she told me that God desired to make me transparent as glass so that the love of God would shine in and through me, and others would know and see God's love for them.

She looked at me, and smiled. She said that during the prayer, she could see in her imagination a window. The wind began to blow and the curtains around the window flowed with the wind. The wind got stronger and the window became brighter and brighter until it became a bright light. She paused, and again looked at me with her bright and beautiful smile. She said, "Bob you are on the right track. Your name is window."

However, she said, "There were strawberry prints on the curtains. Do you have any idea what that might mean?" I told her that I am crazy about strawberries. In fact, earlier that same day for lunch, the restaurant had a special on strawberry pie. If I had eaten my usual lunch, I would not have been hungry enough to eat the pie. So all I had for lunch was a big delicious piece of strawberry pie. She said with her bright eyes and sweet smile, "Isn't God fun?"

I kept thinking, "God, this seems too good to be true. God, you must have me confused with someone else!" Yet, I knew there was no mistake. It had to be true. God even knew what food I liked! When the leader of our prayer meeting prayed with me, she did not know I liked strawberries, and yet she "saw" during our prayer time curtains with strawberry prints. Can God be that personal? One thing for sure, God knows me! I must matter to God! How good it is to be known by God and to know that we are known. I felt so energized and alive. I drove home to my apartment that night with a joy and energy that, up to that time, I have never known or thought possible.

Before I continue, I need to add that I know I did not make this experience happen. It happened to me. It was a gift from God. I know I am nothing special, and yet at the same time, after that experience, I know I am special to God.

If this is true for me, it is true for you, and everyone! We are all special to God! We all matter to God! God knows each of us! God giving you a name may be very new and foreign to you, like it was to me.

In that regard, Richard Rohr, a Franciscan priest, asserts that God gives you two names, your name and God's name. He invites you to listen for that place deep within where God has given you His own name, that name which lovers reveal to one another in intimate moments, where God has told you who He is uniquely for you. It's unlike anybody else's experience of God. You reflect a part of God that no one else will ever reflect.

Learning my name was a moment I will never forget. Knowing that God knows everything about us is so life giving and freeing. Only the One who knows us completely can really love us completely. Knowing we are known by God still changes and challenges my ways of thinking about God, and how I see God, others, and myself.

****

As I close Part One of this book, I am well aware that I have included some experiences that are very surprising; certainly they were surprising to me, and totally unexpected and undeserved. Perhaps some might look upon them with suspicion or skepticism.

I do not know how or why these experiences happen(ed). But I do know that God is continually drawing us closer and closer, and all we can do is stay connected and open like the branches connected to the vine (John 15:7) and SEEK God. "Do not fear little flock, the Father knows what you need, but seek first (the Kingdom of) God, and all these things will be given to you" (Luke 12:31-32). We are asked, first and foremost, not to seek spiritual experiences or look for coincidences, but to seek union with God and then trust.

One of my favorite Scripture passages over the last few years is Jer. 29:11-14: I know the plans I have for you, says the Lord, plans for your welfare, and not for harm, to give you a future of hope. Then when you call upon me and come and pray to me, I will hear you. When you search for me, you will find me; if you seek me [the One Jesus revealed and called God and Father and none other] with all your heart, I will let you find me, says the Lord.

The key to this passage is that we enter into a relationship with God as God is known in Jesus Christ, and this relationship can and will change one's life.

Richard Rohr, OFM, in his book, *Things Hidden: Scripture as Spirituality*, reiterates that we just have to stay on the journey, stay connected, stay in union. When we are connected, synchronicities, coincidences, accidents and providences just happen, and he admittedly says, "I cannot explain the 'chemistry' of it all" (214-5).

I do question the authenticity of experiences of the sacred, either intellectual or experiential, which leave people feeling arrogant, hateful, narcissistic, superior to everyone, and quick to judge, condemn, or exclude. In strong contrast, a sign that we have entered into a relationship with the One who Jesus called God and Father, that we have come close to the sacred, is that this experience will leave us simply grateful and humble.

We see examples of this humility in our Scriptures. John the Baptist, a powerful, bold and brazen man, said when he saw Jesus, "I am not worthy to untie his sandal straps. He must increase, but I must decrease" (John 1:27, 3:30). St. Paul, strong in leadership and courageous in the face of persecution, wrote, "If I have not love, I am nothing" (1 Cor. 13:1). Then there is the marvelous moment when Elizabeth greets Mary, and Elizabeth humbly asks, "Who am I, why has this happened to me, that the mother of my Lord should come to me?" (Luke 1:43). We might rephrase this question, "Who are we that our Lord comes to us?"

When God called Moses to send him to Pharaoh to bring the Israelites out of their slavery in Egypt, Moses said to God, "Who am I that I should go to Pharaoh, and bring the Israelites out of Egypt?" (Ex 3:11).

In short, when we come close to the sacred, we will humbly identify with the meditation that St. Francis held so dearly, "God, who are You? And God, who am I?"

Part Two:

Lord, make me an instrument
of your peace.

Where there is hatred, let me sow love.
Where there is injury, pardon;
Where there is doubt, faith;
Where there is despair, hope;
Where there is darkness, light;
And where there is sadness, joy.

From the peace prayer
attributed to St. Francis of Assisi

CHAPTER 15

The Meeting of Image and the Cross

There are times when we hear a comment or read a statement which, because it rings so clearly and loudly inside of us, we cannot forget. Something inside of us seems to respond with a resounding "Yes!" What we hear contains a great treasure of wisdom and truth, and bears an unexplainable weight of importance and significance, but we really do not know exactly why at the time.

I was a student at Catholic Theological Union (CTU) in Chicago from 1986-1990. One class period, a theology professor veered from his lecture notes, looked at us with all sincerity, and simply said, "Our image of God makes all the difference. Once we get the image of God right, it affects everything. We 'see' differently. Everything changes." Even a true interpretation of Scripture depends on having the proper perspective on the nature of God. Blaise Pascal, a mathematical genius and philosopher, wrote about our image of God, "God made man in his own image and man returned the compliment." It is so natural to unknowingly project onto God whatever image we prefer, grew up with, or learned. I could imagine God saying to me or anyone else, "You have ME confused with some other god."

The theology professor's comment, spoken with such

conviction, echoed within me like wisdom, a simple and profound wisdom and truth. I knew he was right, but I did not realize how right he was, and I did not realize at the time how his statement would become so significant and relevant for me.

Jesus came to help people to know God the Father and for us to experience the Father as Jesus knew and experienced the Father. Jesus desired to reveal to us who the Father is and has always been for all humanity. Jesus entirely embodied the heart of God in human flesh. Jesus became on earth who the Father eternally is and has been for all humankind. A Sunday school child was right in saying, "Jesus is the best picture God has ever taken."

Leslie Weatherhead, a British theologian and clergyman, wrote in the 1900s, "All of God that could be poured into a solitary human being resided in Jesus." However, God, in Jesus, would meet so much resistance that SOMEONE would have to suffer, someone would have to die. But that Someone who died was not among those who resisted God, who resisted God's ways, dreams or hopes for humanity. It was not you or I who would have to die; it was God's Beloved Son!

Jesus embodied God's hopes and dreams and love for all humanity, for our world, for all time. Jesus understood this to be the Kingdom of God, the Reign of God. Jesus gave up His life to proclaim the Kingdom of God. In effect, God is saying to you and me and all creation, "Jesus will reveal to you my love, my forgiveness, my justice and mercy, so people may live in harmony, peace and joy. Jesus will tell you and show you how to live this way and how to build the Kingdom of God, or He will die trying." Jesus gave His all for this mission. His life's mission was to make God's love, forgiveness, mercy, truth, joy, inclusivity, etc. REAL and visible to people, no matter the cost, and what a cost it was! Jesus would not let His message die, so He had to die instead.

If one's image of God, that is, how one thinks of God,

affects everything, I eventually had to face and deal with the reality of the <u>Cross</u>. How compatible was the cross with my image of God that changed so drastically over the years? How do I think about the death of Jesus and feel about His brutal, violent and bloody crucifixion? We know that words fall short to adequately define the significance of the cross, much less what the cross means or how it applies to our lives and faith. How did Jesus' terrible and horrific death ever happen?

The easiest way to explain Jesus' death is to simply say that His death must have been God's will. Maybe that is the easiest way to explain why this awful event happened. Another possible and logical explanation for the cross is that Jesus died on Calvary to fulfill the prophecy of the Old Testament. Jesus just lived out the "script" He was given.

Can I believe that the Father, the One of unconditional love, demanded Jesus to go through this horrible and brutal death to satisfy, appease, and finally to convince Himself, the Father, that we are worth loving and forgiving? Was it Jesus' death that finally satisfied and appeased the Father, and ultimately the gates of heaven were opened so that we could have eternal life?   It became difficult for me to accept the idea that Jesus was born only to die and give His life as a sacrifice for the sins of the world, that God could not forgive us without that event, and that we are ultimately saved when we believe in this.

There is within the Franciscan tradition the position that God became human, not because of the fall or sin of Adam and Eve, our first parents, and not because of our fallen state, but because of our value. The incarnation, God becoming flesh in Jesus, was:

> Plan A, not Plan B. The incarnation was an
> act of love, prior to sin, and was a fitting and
> beautiful action by God, considering God's
> nature as Love. Therefore, why not assert
> the divine intention to become incarnate was

prior to any human failure, and prior to the creation of the world? (Ingham, 31)

The alternative to this position is to believe the incarnation was necessary only in order to make amends, to fix and make up for our mess and wrongdoing, to take care of the punishment that was due us, and to save us from eternal damnation. Therefore, in the eyes of God, in order to solve the problem, someone had to pay the price. Jesus was born to pay the price, and became the perfect sacrifice to satisfy the Father. This is to say, if Adam and Eve had not sinned, perhaps Jesus would not have been necessary, and we would have missed how Jesus revealed the Father, for "if you have seen me [Jesus said], you have seen the Father" (John 14:9).

It seems, given God's nature of love and God's desire to be known, that God would not send His Son to die, but would instead, send His Son to show us how to live. The intention of the incarnation was not so much to fix a problem, save us from eternal damnation, or even to show us how to be more spiritual, but to show us how to become more human and how to relate with God and one another. The "incarnation" was not a one-time act, a thirty-three year experiment in the person of Jesus, or something that happened about two thousand years ago, but rather, the incarnation is ongoing. The Word of God is still looking to take on flesh in you, in me, and in all humankind.

Over the years, I have come to think about the death of Jesus in a much different way. What pleased God was not the brutal and violent death of Jesus, but that Jesus offered His life, His entire life, as a total gift to the Father for all humanity. *Jesus' death was the consequence of his life.* Yes, the death of Jesus was inevitable, and Jesus knew it.

The cross was a clash between love at its best, clashing with sin, selfishness and evil at its worst. Jesus' message of grace, mercy, love, justice, compassion, forgiveness, and inclusivity clashed with sin, selfishness and evil. God was willing to pay the price, to suffer the violence. Without the cross, the full revelation of God is absent. Given the nature of God, God's total self-giving of life and love, the cross was already in the heart of the Father, and Jesus embodied God's nature. Without the cross the full reality of sin and its effects can be easily missed or dismissed. The cross reveals what the sins of humanity are doing to us and to one another.

Without the cross, the message of Jesus would be forgotten or even lose all meaning and significance. We should want to know what Jesus thought was worth dying for. Jesus would not let His message die, so He had to die instead. If Jesus would have agreed with or passively told everyone what they wanted to hear, would they have killed Him? What would have happened if Jesus had said?

- "When life is going really good, if I were you, I would build bigger barns. Forget about everybody else. You have got to watch out for number one."
- "About those people who are different from you: You do not have to care about them. God certainly does not. I would stay away from those sinners. They are not as good as you, and they will not get you anywhere."
- "About this golden rule: Do to others as you would want them to do to you---that is not going to get you anywhere. If they hit you, hit them back, even harder. They will learn their lesson."

If Jesus would have spoken in this way, do you think they would have killed Him? Jesus' death was unavoidable. Jesus could see what was happening. He knew that they had killed all the prophets, and now they wanted to kill Him too. Jesus would not let His message die, so He had to die instead.

CHAPTER 16

Love Willing to Suffer

Jesus died because the religious authorities felt threatened by His message and His ways. They were jealous because so many people were attracted to His message. Jesus died because the political authorities did not want to hear Jesus touted as a King of a different kind of kingdom, the Kingdom of God. Jesus challenged the religious system, and spoke courageously to the political power of His time.

W. Reiser gives a thought provoking explanation for the reason(s) for Jesus' suffering and death. Jesus died because He was resented, betrayed and hated. He was killed out of envy because He threatened political authority and they thought He had taken religion into His own hands. Jesus was betrayed by human sinfulness, but He did not surrender to the power of sin; He surrendered to God. Jesus died, not so much for our sins, but rather *because of our sins*, and the sins of all humanity.

Jesus trusted that God would not allow sin to defeat His mission to forgive sins and to heal human brokenness. The resurrection was God's "YES" to Jesus and validated everything Jesus said and did. Jesus was and is the ultimate and unmistakable "sign of God's unbreakable love for the human race, no matter how wretched or ingrained its sinfulness" (Reiser, 73-74).

There is another level of meaning to this mystery of the cross. I use the word mystery because it is impossible to completely get our minds and hearts around the full meaning and understanding of the cross! On the cross, Jesus truly revealed the Father, namely, who God really is and who God is for us. While the passion, the suffering and death of Jesus described how Jesus died, His passion is much more about His love, revealing the heart and love of the Father. In and through the cross, we see love, love that is willing to suffer. Jesus revealed that our God is a God of suffering love.

Jesus contained in His own heart the love the Father bore for all humanity, for all time. Can you imagine that? Consider how we hurt for another who is hurting or suffering! How our heart aches and breaks for them. I know a mother and father who exemplified this kind of suffering love. One of their children became seriously ill. His breathing was constricted and his condition rapidly declined. A team of doctors hurriedly examined the young boy brought in to the emergency room; they tried to determine the cause of the condition and a proper treatment. The father called me and described the rather frightening details. He asked that I pray for their young son. He said with all sincerity, "You know, if I could take the place of my son, I would do it in a heartbeat."

Imagine if you bore this magnitude and depth of love for everyone. When we too quickly adopt the attitude or belief that God loves some people and hates others, we are deceived. Jesus bore the love of the Father for both those who welcomed and received Him as well as for those who turned away and rejected Him. In Luke 6:32-35, Jesus states:

> "If you love those who love you, what credit can you expect? Even sinners love those who love them. And if you do good to those who do good to you, what credit can you expect? For even sinners do that much. ... Instead,

love your enemies and do good to them. …
you will be children of the Most High, for
he himself is kind to the ungrateful and the
wicked."

Loving your enemies and doing good to them shows a true love, a love that is willing to suffer!

Ron Rolheiser, a columnist and author wrote an article entitled "*Love in a Time of Opposition.*" He wrote about the incredible forgiveness that Jesus offered while He hung upon the cross. Luke 23:34 tells us that Jesus prayed, "Father, forgive them, they do not know what they are doing." The persecutors of Jesus were ignorant of how much they were loved.

In contrast, Jesus knew who He was, God's Son, and how much He was loved. From that awareness, Jesus drew His courage, strength and power to forgive. Like Jesus, we, too, are God's children and are loved that deeply. Like Jesus, we, too, can be that forgiving.

Rolheiser submits that if there was a litmus test, a single particular moral issue to indicate or prove one is a true follower of Jesus, that test would be this: "Can you continue to love those who misunderstand you, who oppose you, who are hostile to you, who hate you and who threaten you—without being paralyzed, calloused or condescending?"

Jesus' death is called a ransom. We read in Mark 10:45, "The Son of Man has not come to be served but to serve—to give his life in ransom for the many." Ransom can mean Jesus paid our debt, which again gives us a rather harsh picture of God; or ransom can simply mean Jesus freed us from sin by showing us how to live free of violence and vengeance, how to love our enemies just as God does, for God makes his sun rise on the evil and good, and sends rain on the just and unjust. (Matt 5:45)

I used to think God was able to forgive because God is so big and powerful and almighty. I now believe with all my heart that what makes God so big, powerful, great and almighty is exactly because of God's eagerness and capacity to forgive, to show mercy, and to revive and restore us. Recently I saw a picture of the Sacred Heart of Jesus hanging in a church. At the bottom of the picture was the caption, "If you believe, you will see the power of my heart." Jesus shows us where the power of God resides. The power of God is to "know" the heart and love of the Father for all humanity. Jesus embodied this power of the heart. If we did not hear or see it in the way Jesus lived, we probably could not see it in the way He died.

How do we BECOME LIKE JESUS in light of the mystery of the cross? Jesus did not return violence for violence. Though He was hated, He did not hate in return; though He was crucified, He did not crucify in return; though He was killed, He did not kill in return.

Henri Nouwen, a renowned author of many books on spirituality, wrote something so simple, so profound, and so extremely important. Nouwen believed that all the gospels, all Scripture, is meant to lead us to these three little words: BECOME LIKE JESUS. These three little words haunt me. It is not enough to merely believe in Him, and merely think this belief is sufficient to assure one's personal salvation and eternal life, that is, to get to heaven. Unless we become like Jesus, life is business as usual and nothing much changes.

How do we BECOME LIKE JESUS in light of the mystery of the cross? Jesus did not return violence for violence. Though He was hated, He did not hate in return; though He was crucified, He did not crucify in return; though He was killed, He did not kill in return.

If Jesus would have responded in kind, which is the way the "world" generally responds, we would have no reason to be Christian, to hold up His life, death and resurrection as the core of our belief and faith. There would be no such thing as Christianity because we would have nothing to proclaim. Such a worldly response would have been just more and more of the same. Jesus did not proclaim a Gospel of revenge; He proclaimed a Gospel of reconciliation.

CHAPTER 17

Noticing What Is in the Middle

Jesus retained the love of the Father for Himself and all humanity. He hung in the middle, not on one side or the other side. Amid great opposition and division, Jesus hung in the middle on the cross, trying to reconcile the opposites. When you try to build a bridge between two sides, you will be walked on by both sides. Jesus "paid the price," not to the Father, but for being in the middle and trying to reconcile all things in Himself no matter the cost, even to the point of shedding His blood on the cross. Wherever there are opposites, we need a middle. A middle helps us to focus on what really matters and to realize that this life is no longer about us, but instead, this life is about all of us.

One day, I received a call from a hospital in Mississippi where I lived at the time. There was a patient whose health was rapidly declining. Though it was not an emergency, he wanted a priest to pray with him and anoint him.

I rushed to the hospital, found his room number, and entered the room. To my surprise, the room was empty, no patient, not even a hospital bed. I noticed a man in the room. I walked over to him and introduced myself. I told him, "I received a call from the hospital that a patient by the name of Vince wanted to see a priest." So, looking around, I said, "I must be in the wrong room." He assured me that I was in the right room.

He introduced himself to me as Sid and informed me that Vince was his uncle. Vince was not in the room because he had been taken for more tests. I told Sid that I would go and visit other patients in the hospital and come back later. Sid replied, "My uncle has been gone for a long time. They should bring him back any time now." I decided to stay, and I am glad that I did.

Sid and I began to talk as we waited for Vince to return. I do not know how long Sid and I talked in that hospital room, but I do know that I thoroughly enjoyed our conversation, and I know the feeling was mutual. Sid was a Baptist. In some regions, for some people, Baptists and Catholics do not mix very well. We talked about our faith, about our relationship with God, and how this relationship changed our lives in so many ways. Sid talked about how much he loved, appreciated and admired his uncle, and how close they were. Finally two nurses wheeled Vince into the room. He was in his hospital bed accompanied by the I.V. pole draped with numerous medicines.

The three of us, Vince, Sid, and myself, talked at length about Vince's health, his family, and their relationship as uncle and nephew. I admired how free they were to express their love and gratefulness for each other. I asked Vince about the anointing and prayer he requested. The Catholic Church offers this anointing to those of poor health, be it physical, emotional, spiritual or psychological. Vince affirmed that he would like to receive this anointing. I stood on one side of the bed and Sid stood on the other side. *In the middle* lay Vince in his hospital bed.

I began to anoint Vince. Out of the corner of my eye, I saw Sid gradually step back and move a considerable distance from his uncle's bed. My first thought was, this Baptist must be uncomfortable, and understandably so, because this anointing is really a Catholic prayer and ritual.

But for some reason, I could not continue while Sid was standing at such a distance. Something was not right. What mattered most was Vince. Vince was the reason we were there. I told Sid and Vince that their love and respect for each other was so obvious, so admirable. I looked at Sid, now some distance from the bed, and invited him to come closer and join us for this time of prayer for Vince. I invited Sid to say or pray anything he wished.

Our time of prayer was absolutely heartwarming, not only because of the love they expressed for each other during the prayer, but also any differences or distance between Baptist and Catholic simply faded away. We were one, and all that mattered at that time was the well being of Vince. Here Sid and I were, a Catholic and a Baptist praying together, brought together by his hurting uncle in the middle.

My relationship with Sid and Vince grew closer during the few next weeks. Vince's health weakened and he was placed under hospice care. We continued to meet numerous times around Vince's bedside. Meanwhile Sid and I met to talk about and plan the inevitable funeral service. I officiated at the service. Sid proclaimed the Scriptures. But all the while, I was grateful to Vince for teaching me so much about the reconciling middle that brings opposites together.

You and I know that our Christian denominations and even the various world religions will never come together by discussing our philosophies, our theologies, our beliefs, our structures, our rituals and practices, our ideologies. But we can come together when and where it matters, let go of our differences, forget about ourselves for a while, bridge the gaps or chasms that exist, and come together for the sake of others. Can we take courage to place in the middle the needs that will compel us to be compassionate as our Heavenly Father is compassionate, so that the arguing, the conflicts, the rivalries and the wars will cease, and the greatest needs will be served?

During the Christmas season of 2010, two seemingly opposing groups of people came together. Jews and Muslims in the Detroit area united Christmas Day to serve the community. About fifty Muslims joined several hundred Jews at sites and served food to the homeless, sorted through books for sale to benefit literacy education, and took the elderly to a Christmas Eve service.

The prophet Isaiah offers a vision, an image of what God hopes and dreams for all creation. We may think this vision sounds more like a fairy tale or something out of a children's book. From Isaiah we read:

> Then the wolf shall be a guest of the lamb,
> and the leopard shall lie down with the kid;
> the calf and the young lion shall browse
> together, with a little child to guide them.
> The cow and the bear shall be neighbors,
> together their young shall rest; the lion shall
> eat hay like the ox. The baby shall play by
> the cobra's den, and the child lay his hand on
> the adder's liar. There shall be no harm or
> ruin on all my holy mountain; for the earth
> shall be filled with the knowledge of the Lord.
> (Isa. 11: 6-9)

This particular passage is most often depicted as the lion and the lamb lying down together in peace. Can this happen? How is this possible? After all, often two neighbors, two co-workers, or even two members of the same family cannot get along.

Is this vision just a fairy tale? No. The prophet presents these images as God's dream, hope and desire for all humanity, for all time. For Jesus, this is the Kingdom of God. The Kingdom of God or the Reign of God is not to be projected into the future (Heaven) after we breathe our last breath, but it is this world here and now, not a later or future world.

When we pray the Lord's Prayer as directed in Matt. 6:9-10, "Thy Kingdom come, thy will be done, on earth, as it is in heaven," we are praying for the coming of God's kingdom on earth here and now. I like the comment that is quoted by so many, making the original author impossible to know, "Heaven is in good shape; earth is where the problems are." We pray that the Kingdom of God may be here on earth, which is the dream and desire of God.

The Kingdom of God breaks into this world whenever and wherever we act as God would act. In this Kingdom, opposites can co-exist and live in harmony. These opposites could include, for example, people of different world religions and religious persuasions, different communities of faith within a denomination or among different denominations of the Christian church. God's vision for our world is to bring together people of different political persuasions, religions, cultures, social and income status, etc. Impossible, you say? It would seem impossible given our present national and international conflicts we see and hear every day in the news.

One evening on a television news show, the host interviewed a husband and wife about their living situation. This retired couple faced dire financial and health conditions. The wife suffered from cancer and they had no health insurance. They looked throughout their home for any items they could sell in a garage sale, and they put these items aside in boxes. Their last resort and slim hope was to sell these little items and have some money to make at least a minimal payment so they could continue to buy her cancer medicine and she could receive her cancer treatments. Without this medicine and treatments, she would surely die.

They both said that after their next garage sale, they would not have anything more to sell to generate any income. The perfect place for this couple was in the middle, in the middle as health insurance companies, lawmakers of all political parties and backgrounds, and leaders of our country discussed health care. This couple and their desperate situation might have influenced the discussion about health care reform, or at least affected the tenor of the discussion.

When there is opposition between two sides, I believe God is in the middle, where God has always been. God is in the middle trying to bring together, trying to reconcile the two opposing sides. Can this mean that as we move closer to each other, to the other side, we also move closer to God? As we move further away from the other side and ramp up the opposition, are we also moving further away from God?

Which best represents the way of the Kingdom of God? Are we to be on this side or the other side, or in the middle? When one side believes "God is on my side," and the other side believes "God is my side," and we know that there is only one God, each side can too quickly demonize the other. No progress is made and, in the name of God, hatred and even violence can break out. Where do we imagine God is? Where is the place of the Church, which represents Christ, in this scheme?

But I also offer this caution and reminder. If God is on any side, we know clearly from our Scriptures and from the life of Jesus that God favors the little nobodies, the people who "fall through the cracks," the weak and vulnerable, the powerless and the poor, the ones taken advantage of who, in Scripture, are described as the widow and the orphan (Isa. 1:17, Ps. 146:9).

Returning to the vision and message of Isaiah, do you think such reconciliation is possible? Perhaps a better question is: Is this *your* hope, *your* vision for our world? If not, why not? We cannot make this vision and dream, which is God's dream, happen on our own power. The lion and the lamb can only be together, can only co-exist together, because of the One who is in the middle bringing them together.

We must be honest with ourselves. If this vision, this image, is not our image, we must at least honestly admit it.

If this vision and dream of God is not becoming more and more a reality, chances are the One, or the Spirit of the One in the middle is missing, or is being ignored or even silenced. This picture presents the vision of Isaiah. Is this your vision too?

The Lion and the Lamb
Copyright 1990 by The Order of Saint Benedict, Inc.
Published by Liturgical Press,
Collegeville,Minnesota.
Reprinted with permission.

CHAPTER 18

Show Us What That Looks Like

Several years ago I attended a Franciscan gathering, the theme of which was reconciliation and forgiveness. Our weekend included some very talented speakers known worldwide, and who were also successful authors. After a great presentation on the subject of forgiveness, one speaker asked us the following question: "We all agree on the importance of forgiveness as presented in our Scriptures, especially the Gospels. My question is, If forgiveness is so important, and we would even say essential, why do we see so little forgiveness?" It was a great question.

The majority of our Franciscans have a high level of education; therefore, we tried to answer his question with very logical and educated answers. After each of our answers, he said, "That is true, but I do not think that is the real reason." Finally after we exhausted all our answers and guesses, he simply said, "I believe the real answer to the question of why we see so little forgiveness is that *we don't see forgiveness modeled*. Therefore, we do not know what forgiveness looks like, sounds like, feels like, or how it is done." I thought his insight was absolutely brilliant.

Can this insight mean that our true calling is to model, to make visible and tangible the life, mission and message of Jesus through our own lives, thereby revealing the Father's hope and desire for all humanity? Is this the purpose and goal of all religion(s)? Is it possible to simply say that God wants us to be images and models of Himself? How can we model the love, compassion, truth, justice, forgiveness, mercy, prophetic word, inclusivity, etc. of God, and make these real and present through our own lives? How can we be instruments of God, demonstrating God's presence to others? By modeling the Christian life in and through our own lives, we make God's presence in today's world visible and tangible. Our lives and our example help others to see and believe how the Gospel is believable and livable.

Can you imagine a world where there is so much light that darkness does not stand a chance? We all agree there is too much "darkness" in our world. However the problem is magnified because there is not enough light. When we light a candle in a dark room, the candlelight does not lose its brightness. The dark room becomes lighter and brighter. The only thing that cuts through darkness is light.

In a speech titled "Strength to Love" given in 1963, Martin Luther King, using the symbols of darkness and light, spoke a powerful message, "Darkness cannot drive out darkness; only light can do that. Hate cannot drive out hate; only love can do that." We must be careful, vigilant and alert when these two symbols of light and darkness become confused with each other, when darkness becomes light and light becomes darkness. Examples of such confusion are the following: there is good greed and bad greed; good hate and bad hate; good violence and bad violence; good bombing and bad bombing; good killing and bad killing.

It is up to us, we who say we are believers or followers of Jesus, to keep the darkness at bay by living lives that manifest the light of the Lord's goodness, justice, peace, mercy, forgiveness, welcome etc. When we become that kind of light and that kind of truth, the darkness and deceptions will fade away. To become a light for the world, it is essential that we stay close to the source of Light who is Christ because our light can grow dim and we do not even realize the change.

We can easily become accustomed to the gradual darkness that sets in without even recognizing the change as darkness. As a young boy and teenager growing up on the farm, my four older brothers and I enjoyed playing ball in the yard in the evening after we finished our chores. One batted and the others fielded. We took turns hitting and fielding, and played ball into the late evening. As the sun set and the evening grew darker, our eyes adjusted to the dark.

Eventually, one of our parents would call out from the house, "You kids better stop playing ball. It's too dark. You can't even see the ball any more!" Finally we stopped and went into the house. When we got into our well-lit house, we saw just how dark it really was outside. Someone had to call our attention to how dark it really had gotten. It had not seemed that dark while we were outside. We had gradually adjusted to the darkness.

It is obvious we cannot see as we should when we are in the dark. Likewise, when we look through the darkness of our fears, angers, hurts, envy, resentments, revenge, insecurity, perhaps feeling that we do not have enough or that we are not enough, we cannot "see" God, our world or ourselves correctly. But, maybe equally or even more problematic, we cannot see our own goodness, our own God-given inner beauty, abilities, gifts, etc. When we gradually blend into the darkness around us, we have little or nothing to say and nothing to witness to as Christian people. Our light has become dimmed.

Jesus is the visible image of the invisible God; we are also called to be a visible image of the invisible God, thus making God visible. Jesus did not come to keep us out of hell, or necessarily come to get us into heaven; Jesus came to get heaven into us and thereby create a human family who reflects something of the nature of God for others.

Jesus is told, "Your mother and your brothers and

sisters are outside asking for you." Jesus responds, "Who are my mother, my brothers and sisters? Whoever does the will of God are my brother and sister and mother" (Mark 3: 31-35). God wants us to create a new family.

To model and make present God or the Spirit of God requires much more, and is much more challenging and rewarding than simply believing this or believing that about God. As a very elderly and wise woman who was close to one hundred years old said to me, "You doesn't have to believe what I says, but you does have to believe what I does." Maybe she spoke with bad grammar, but she spoke with good wisdom. How we live is the message.

Several years ago I was the pastor of a church in Mississippi. I invited anyone of any denomination to join our Church. For a number of weeks, I invited people through verbal and written communication. During that time I received only one phone call. A woman, Dorothy, called and told me she was interested. I thanked her for calling and told her that I would call her back when we officially began the instructions and process. I thought I was off to a good start and expected more calls and inquiries. I was wrong. Weeks passed by. It was time to begin the instructions. I had only one person interested, Dorothy.

I called Dorothy and told her that she was the only one who called, so I offered her an option. She could come to the church, or I could meet with her in her home. She really liked the idea to meet in her home. So, one evening, I packed up all my stuff and arrived at her house where I met Dorothy for the first time. She warmly greeted me and invited me to come inside.

Her house was simple, extremely poor and old looking, with walls really in need of a coat of paint. We sat at her kitchen table and talked, trying to get to know each other better. As we talked, I pulled my stuff out of my brief case and placed it in an orderly fashion on the table. I had brought all my instructional materials, brochures, informational pamphlets, and my Bible. I was ready.

As we talked, a sound came from the next room. Dorothy hurriedly pushed herself away from the table and rushed into the next room. I heard a suction-like sound come from the next room. Eventually Dorothy returned to the table, sat down and apologized repeatedly for the interruption. I asked her what happened and if everything was all right. She answered, "That was for my daughter, Audrey. Would you like to meet Audrey?" I replied, "I would."

I was not ready for what happened next. I walked into the living room, and on the couch sat a young woman, clearly physically challenged. Pillows braced both sides of her, a tube was inserted into her stomach area, she was unable to talk, and could only make sounds. Dorothy said to Audrey, "Audrey, this is Fr. Bob." Audrey's face lit up with a huge smile.

Dorothy and I stayed in the living room with Audrey for a while and then returned to the kitchen table. Dorothy again apologized for the interruption. She invited me to continue where I left off. Instead, I asked Dorothy about the suction sound. Dorothy explained that she has to clear out any blockages in Audrey's feeding tube. I said to Dorothy, "You must be so attuned to that sound that it even wakes you out of your sleep in the middle of the night." She said to me something I will never forget, "Oh, I don't sleep in my bed; Audrey sleeps on my lap." I was stunned.

I needed to understand what she just said. Dorothy said, "I sit up on the couch and sleep, and Audrey sleeps with her head on my lap. When she was born, she was born with very little brain tissue. The doctors did not give her any hope of living. Audrey is now thirty two years old." I was speechless. After a period of silence, Dorothy asked me, "So, what were we talking about?" I said, with a sense of irony while paging through my Bible, "I was going to tell you what it means to be a Christian." That sounded so out of place and hollow. All my information that I had wanted to present to Dorothy that night seemed suddenly trivial and irrelevant. I told her, "I should be the one who sits at your feet and learns from you what it takes to be a Christian."

Dorothy went through the process and officially joined the Church at Easter. She told the congregation, "All my life I took care of everybody, my father, my mother, my daughter. I finally took care of myself. All my life I kept hearing that God loves me. Now I don't just hear it, I know it. Now I know God loves me!" She said this with such conviction, depth, and radiant love that many in the church could not hold back their tears, including me. I knew immediately in my heart why Dorothy was the only one who responded to my invitation, to my appeal. Dorothy needed to be the only one because everything we did was all done for her.

Both Dorothy and Audrey died a number of years later. First Dorothy passed away, and then Audrey shortly after. I will never forget Dorothy, my time with her, the way she modeled Christianity, and how she lived her life as a Christian. I had come to Dorothy's house armed with a lot of words, both the printed word and my own prepared words. However, Dorothy silenced my words, and instead showed me what being Christ-like looked like. Dorothy lived and modeled the light and Gospel of Christ, the light of incredible love and compassion.

CHAPTER 19

Not Only Dying, but Rising, Too

Looking at my experience with Dorothy and Audrey, I believe that the cross and Jesus' invitation and exhortation to take up our cross are to be understood as a way of life and a way to live. I hear people describe in many different ways the cross(es) they carry. Some say their cross is a disease, a physical limitation, chronic pain or something similar. Others describe the cross they carry as being another person who causes them hardship or some type of suffering.

We read in our Scriptures that Jesus said not just once but several times, "Whoever does not carry the cross and follow me cannot be my disciple" (Luke 14: 27). The cross of Jesus, and following Jesus, necessarily includes a dying and a rising. We, too, are invited into that pattern of dying and rising.

This pattern of dying and rising is the pattern for a disciple. We are invited to die to ourselves, that is, to deny ourselves and rise to a new way of being and "seeing." Perhaps the following examples will help us understand what that means in practical circumstances. A husband and wife have just experienced the birth of their first child. While feeling exhilarated and excited about the arrival of their newborn, they are both exhausted, physically and emotionally, and anxious to bring their newborn home. Finally the parents and newborn are home from the hospital and it is their first night together. They hope to get some overdue and well-earned sleep. But just as they fall asleep, from the next room comes a cry from their newborn.

The husband and wife, now a father and mother, must make a choice. Their bed feels so good, the sleep is so wonderful and needed. They have a choice. They can stay in bed and wait for their newborn to hopefully cry him/herself to sleep. Or they must *die* to the desire to stay in bed and get that well-deserved sleep, and *rise* to take care of the need that is before them.

Another example of dying and rising is the following: You have a certain opinion or bias about a particular matter and you hold strongly to your opinion. However, you hear some new information, some new facts, or have some experience that challenges your opinion. You have a choice. You can hold to your old opinion or bias, even though it is very faulty and now clearly false, or you can die to your old opinion, your old way of seeing, and rise to a new understanding. When we refuse to live in this pattern of dying and rising, selfishness or being shortsighted will prevail.

Jesus did not just talk about dying and rising, He lived it. Finally, so we would not miss it, He showed this dying and rising in His very body. Jesus showed us that with every dying, there is a rising. This is the pattern of our life. This is the life pattern of a disciple, a follower of Jesus.

There are so many ways to talk about this process of dying and rising. Somewhere, sometime, we have to find that person, that action, that inspiration to which we give ourselves over with our whole heart. This surrender exhausts the pre-occupation we have with ourselves, softens our hearts, frees us, invites us to "let go of our lives," and brings us strangely and wonderfully to our new selves, our real selves. To use Biblical language, "For those who want to save their life will lose it, and those who lose their life for my sake will find it" (Matt. 16:25).

A few years ago I joined my family for Thanksgiving Day and our holiday dinner. While we were setting the table we decided as a family, without letting our mother know, that we would deliberately place our mother in a position at the dinner table where she could not get up and take care of everybody during the meal. We pinned her between the table and the wall. We often jokingly asked our mother if she ever ate a hot meal in her life. During meals, she always got up from the table to get more food when the supply on the table was running low, or would ask if anyone wanted more potatoes, meat, salad, dessert, you name it. But this time, she was unable get up from the table. She could finally just sit, eat and enjoy her meal, or so we thought. Man! Did that backfire!

Mom was so uneasy during that entire meal. She was anxious and felt out of place. We all felt her discomfort. She did not enjoy that Thanksgiving dinner at all. Never again, we thought. We actually thought we were doing a good deed for our mother. Little did we realize that we prevented her from being herself. Taking care of us at the table and serving us is who she was. She had given herself over to this life of service, and she could not be herself if she was not able to serve. She could not be her best self, her real self. Seeing her in this way, we only learned to appreciate her more.

CHAPTER 20

Being Saved and Changed

There is a story of a man who was stopped on the street by a young man who was very enthusiastic about his faith. The young man had just given his life to the Lord, and he felt excited about being "born again." He stopped the man on the street and asked him, "Brother, are you saved?" The man did not respond, but instead, pulled out a piece of paper and wrote on it. He handed the paper to the stranger and said, "Instead of taking my word to answer your question, here are the names and addresses of my family, neighbors, and the people I work with. Ask them if they think I am saved." The man was placing this language of being saved into the context of observable and real life. For example, one who is saved, born again, transformed or whatever terminology you prefer, might display the following changes:

- From power-driven, ego-driven, control-driven to a desire to serve, to give;
- From selfish and greedy to generous, giving, attentive to the needs of others;
- From bitter and resentful to forgiving and peaceful;

- From arrogant, self-righteous, sarcastic and cynical to humble and accepting;
- From fearful and hateful to loving and courageous;
- From being controlled by materialism /consumerism to simplicity of lifestyle;
- From an eye-for-an-eye justice, violence and revenge to seeking reconciliation and non-violence;
- From jealous to grateful and thankful;
- From excluding, separating, dividing to including, accepting, welcoming and hospitality;
- From noise and distraction to comfort with quiet, silence, peacefulness, and solitude.

A changed life is the greatest sign of the Spirit of God at work.

As W. Reiser wrote, "There is a transforming power in love; we are changed to the degree that we love. We become newly made the more we allow love to claim our soul, our liberty, our mind, our strength" (30). We are transformed in the process of dying and rising. We are "saved" in the process. We are saved from ourselves and our selfish or self-centered tendencies, our destructive or self-destructive actions, thoughts and attitudes.

We will have to give an account of our life. Life cannot continue on and on as it is. I am unsure who originated this saying, but it is applicable here, "Our life is a gift from God. What we make of our life or who we become is our gift to God." I have come to believe that the great question(s) we will be asked at the time of judgment will be rather simple, and the criteria for our answer(s) will be quite uncomplicated. I believe the great questions we will be asked at the end of our life, or at the time of judgment, will be something along the lines of, "Were the lives of others better because of your own?" In other words, "How did you help the lives of others to be better because of your own life?"

We are told through our American culture that we are entitled to the good life by right. However, as followers of Christ, we are called to live a life that is good. So the question becomes, how do we know if our life was good? The answer for a Christian would hinge on whether or not our life was good for others. It seems all that God asks of us is that our lives produce good. We are accountable for our life, and God has every right to ask us, "What good did you bring to the lives of others? What have you done with my created world, the world I created and love and provided for you?"

I have come to believe, though this may sound too simplistic, that the criteria on which our lives are and will be evaluated is rather uncomplicated. In addition, I am convinced that we have made religion far too complicated. When Bishop Ken Untener (1937-2004) ordained me a Deacon of the Church in 1990, I understood the importance and significance of what he said. I will never forget his wise, insightful, and profound words:

> The religious leaders of Jesus' time made religion complex, and they considered people's lives to be simple. Jesus comes into the fray, and says, 'Do not tell the people their lives are simple and make religion complex; but respect the complexity of their lives while telling them the simple truths of our faith.'

CHAPTER 21

Doing Good, but "Just Passing Through"

One of the great qualities and beauty of Scripture is that it provides a larger context. Scripture itself can be another type of eyeglasses, another lens, to help us see and understand from another perspective. The Scripture passage from Matt. 21:33-46, the parable of the vineyard and the wicked servants, might help to simplify what is expected of us as followers of Jesus, as people of God. God made a great investment in a vineyard. God did everything necessary to make his vineyard fruitful but was disappointed in return. This parable represents God's repeated appeals through the prophets and finally through his Son.

Relating this passage to our contemporary time, this parable becomes more relevant and meaningful. The owner of the vineyard is God. The tenants are the people, you and I and all humanity for all time, past, present and to come. The servants are the prophets. The son that the owner sends is Jesus. The vineyard is our created world, our environment, the planet earth as well as the people who live on this earth. God has provided everything for us.

We are the tenants, not the owners. God wants us to

take care of one another and to act as tenants and stewards of our environment, our created world, and to live lives that produce good (fruit). In the words of the prophet Isaiah, the partial source of this parable in Matthew, "[the owner, God] expected the vineyard to yield fine grapes: but wild grapes were all it yielded" (Isa. 5: 2). The tenants forgot that they were the tenants, not the owners. Whatever we rent, whether it is an apartment, tool, house or vehicle, we do not own it. Yet we are expected and obligated to treat what we rent as our own.

As tenants, we are a global community that consists of many cultures and religions. Given the brief period of our individual lives within the overall span of history, we are to make this world a better place for people now, and for all who will come after us. Because of your life and my life, how are the lives of others better?

This question or criteria on which to evaluate, judge or base a person's accountability is a "Kingdom of God" question or criteria that cuts through all the divisions, categories, and walls we have created. These divisions, categories and walls include our cultures, ethnic groups, political affiliations, (Democrat, Republican, etc.), Christian religion and the various denominations within the Christian Church, world religions, young and old, rich and poor, and everything in between, even between believers and non-believers. Will we be judged on how faithful or loyal we were to our particular culture, or political affiliation? Or will we be judged on how we *as a particular* culture, religion, political affiliation etc. did or did not make life better for others? It is a Kingdom question and it applies to everyone. Everyone is going to be held accountable.

The Scripture passage in Luke 7:1-10 clearly highlights the importance of what we contribute to the lives of others. In this passage, a Roman centurion, a Gentile, has a slave who is ill and near death. The centurion, who helped build a Jewish synagogue, sent elders of the Jews to Jesus to ask Jesus to come and save the life of his slave.

We already see a breaking down of divisions on several levels: the difference of religious beliefs did not separate the centurion and the Jews; the Gentile centurion had a good relationship with the Jews, and the Jews had a good relationship with the centurion; Jesus did not exclude anyone who was different from His own ethnicity or religious practice.

Jesus heard about the centurion and admired his humility and his concern for the well being of the slave. The centurion did not feel worthy to come to Jesus, however, "Say but the word, and let my servant be healed." Jesus was amazed. The centurion was a powerful man, a person of authority. He could easily find another slave. Why should he care about this slave? Jesus turned to the crowd made up of Jews and exclaimed, "I tell you, not even in Israel have I found such faith." Jesus called it like He saw it. This centurion simply cared about people; he let go of categories, rank, titles and status, ethnic lines and different religious beliefs.

We do not know what kind of faith the centurion had, nor do we know what set of beliefs he held. But still Jesus is amazed by his *faith*. It seems Jesus is pointing out to the Jews and to us, "This is what I am talking about! This is what I've been waiting to see!" Jesus exclaimed that He had not found such faith among His own people. He recognized the centurion's extraordinary compassion for his servant. This centurion simply cared about human beings! This centurion saw and acted beyond all the categories of religion, class and power. Given Jesus' reaction, can one sign of true faith simply be how we treat one another as human beings?

CHAPTER 22

I Thought I Could Live Like This Forever; What Was I Thinking?

The opposite of paying attention to others is, of course, to be self-centered. Clearly the centurion, from the previous chapter, paid attention to the need that was before him. Fr. Eugene Walsh, a priest and liturgist, calls this paying attention or hospitality. Fr. Walsh believes that:

> Hospitality expresses the best kind of love we would hope to find in Christian community and within Christians themselves. Hospitality takes time. It takes deliberate, conscious effort. When we pay attention, we stop being preoccupied with ourselves and make the effort to get out of ourselves and be interested in the other. (17).

I was once asked, "Do you love as you could or should? Why or why not?" These are great questions because they place the focus exactly where the focus should be, namely upon relationships. In good and healthy human relationships, there is a flow of love and friendship, a receiving and a giving of love and friendship. These questions led me to look at where in my life I may have blocked this flow or what may be blocking this flow of life, love, and friendship.

When selfishness reaches serious proportions, it can become deadly to spiritual and human growth. When selfishness and self-centeredness become the only way one looks at life, it appears that there is no need to repent, no need to change. Though God's love is available and present, selfish people do not open the door to God's love. In a sense, they have hardened their conscience, hardened their hearts. There is no self-examination. There is no listening to one's life or any others.

It is hard to imagine anyone becoming so hardened and calloused to the point where they could ignore their conscience. People steeped in selfishness no longer care to ask, or even seem capable of asking themselves, "What is this way of life, my attitudes, actions or choices doing to me? What kind of person am I becoming?"

An episode in the cartoon Garfield the Cat contains a simple story with a profound message. One cold winter night Garfield looked out the window and saw Odie, the dog, peering through the window. Garfield thought to himself, "This is horrible. Here I am in the comfort of a warm house, well fed, and there is Odie outside begging to get in, cold and hungry. I can't stand it anymore! I just can't stand it!" So at that he went over to the window and closed the curtain.

I told this story at a church service. After I returned home from the service, I received a phone call. It was a church member, a husband and father, who had attended the service. He told me, "Man! After that story, when I got home, I wanted to rip down all the curtains from my windows!"

We have a story in our Scriptures of a rich man and a poor man named Lazarus (Luke 16:19-31). The rich man flaunted his wealth and reputation. He loved to dress in purple garments and fine linen, and dine sumptuously each day. Meanwhile, lying at his door was a poor man named Lazarus, covered with sores, who would gladly have eaten his fill of the scraps that fell from the rich man's table. Eventually both died. The poor man is carried by the angels to the bosom of Abraham. The rich man was buried and, from the netherworld, he was in torment.

Years ago, after reading this parable, I would have concluded that the poor man, Lazarus, went to his eternal reward and the rich man to his eternal punishment, or as the parable uses the term, "torment." I looked at life as if it was a test and God was the scorekeeper. The score of this test of life was *pass* or *fail*. I assumed God sent those who passed the test of life to their eternal reward, heaven. Those who failed the test of life, God sent to their eternal punishment, hell. In effect, God became an "Eternal Torturer."

I now refuse to believe God is the Eternal Torturer, especially now that my image of God has changed so drastically. God does not want us to live in torment. If God does not want us to live in torment, two questions arose for me: Where does the torment come from? And what is this torment? Once we remove the religious trappings from this parable, a new perspective, a new "seeing" becomes possible.

Imagine that there is someone who is so self-absorbed, self-centered and self-preoccupied like the rich man in the parable. When death comes, he is no longer able to "satisfy the self or ego" or to use others and everything else for his own gratification, advancement or pleasure. When this is no longer possible after death, it *will feel like torment*. In this state, he lives eternally frustrated or tormented because he is unable to fill his insatiable selfish need. If all that mattered to him during his life was his reputation, social status, power, title, economic class, popularity or fame, when he dies all this will die with him.

All that really matters is who he has become.

Jesus taught more about the danger of wealth, riches, power and possessions than any other single moral topic in all the four Gospels. He did not speak necessarily in a negative way against wealth, riches, possessions, etc., *per se*, but against the danger of how they can adversely affect us and who we can become if these become the focus of our lives. Interestingly, in contrast, those we call saints need less and less to be happy.

Ron Rolheiser asks the following with great insight into the issue of rich and poor, "Does God love the rich less?" In his column entitled "Does God Have Favorites?" Rolheiser writes:

> For Jesus, there are only two kinds of persons: Those who are poor and those who are not yet in touch with their own poverty. And it's not that God prefers us to be poor and loves us better when we are poor. Rather it's when we are poor and in touch with our poverty, we more easily invite in love, both that of God and that of others. God does favor the poor, but, if we truly know our own condition, that's all of us."

How do we know when we become self-absorbed and that this preoccupation with self is taking over our life? We become "deaf and blind" to anyone else, and we no longer "pay attention." We begin to see people as we desire them to be, to satisfy our needs, or perhaps to see others as a threat against satisfying our wants. When we use people and love things, versus loving people and using things, something is taking us over.

Is it possible that God is trying to save us from the illusion that we can live in a self-absorbed manner forever, even after death? The more self-absorbed we are, the more it will feel like torment. Putting the parable into this context, we see that God is not playing some kind of religious game with us. God is trying to save us from ourselves.

We do need a Savior! God wants to save us from the *illusion* we can live a self-absorbed, self-centered life forever, even after death. There is a telling and true statement I read some time ago, "No one loves his alarm clock." But we all know we need an alarm clock to wake us up and get us moving in the right direction. This parable is like an alarm clock. This parable can literally save us, that is, save us from ourselves, if we wake up and pay attention now.

The incredible part of this story is how selfish and self-centered the rich man became. In the parable, even after death, the rich man, in his torment, wanted to treat Lazarus like a servant. "Father Abraham, send Lazarus to bring a drop of water to cool my tongue." How amazing and sad! Abraham said to the rich man, "Between us and you a great chasm is established to prevent anyone from crossing who might wish to go from our side to yours or from your side to ours."

Abraham did not establish this chasm. God did not establish this chasm. The rich man established the chasm during his life. The great sin the rich man committed was that he did not pay attention to other people. He ignored Lazarus, and he and his selfishness created a chasm, a divide that became impassible.

The rich man created this chasm by the way he chose to live. His accumulated choices moved him in the direction of being extremely selfish and self-centered. His individual actions and choices formed the overall narrative or pattern of his life.

This chasm is not only created through choices by individuals, but also on a collective level. The prophet Isaiah shows us that God has little patience with those who take advantage of the vulnerable, the defenseless, the powerless and the poor.

Woe to those who enact unjust decrees, who
compose oppressive legislation to deny justice
to the weak and to cheat the humblest of my
people of fair judgment, to make widows their
prey and to rob the orphan. What will you
do on the day of punishment, when disaster
comes from far away? To whom will you
run for help and where will you leave your
riches, to avoid squatting among the captives
or falling among the slain? After all this, his
anger is not spent. No, his hand is still raised.
(Is 10:1-4)

In other words, do we make life harder and more
difficult for those whose lives are already hard and difficult
so that those whose lives are easy and comfortable will have
more ease and comfort? Those who have never experienced
a moment of want in their lives can rarely relate, identify, or
empathize with the vulnerable, the hurting, or the suffering.

The rich man did finally show some concern for
someone other than himself when he asked Abraham to send
Lazarus to his five brothers to warn them to change their
ways so they do not end up like him. So who are we in this
parable? We are not Lazarus, the poor man. We are not the
rich man. We are the five brothers. The rich man wanted to
warn his brothers to save them from living the same illusion
he lived.

Several years ago our province needed to vote for
our next leader. Within the community there was a very
talented, gifted, intelligent and well-known young man who
appeared to be a "rising star." This man wanted to be the
leader of the community.

When the time to vote came closer, I said to an elderly
priest in the community, "I don't know why they even have
to vote. We already know who will win. Everyone will
vote for him." The elderly priest said to me, "I hope not."
Surprised by his comment, I asked, "What do you mean?" I

will never forget his response. He said, "Because he has not suffered enough." He continued, "He would never be able to identify with this community. He could not relate with compassion, patience or understanding to the elderly, the sick, the aging, the troubled, to this community of men with such a wide range of personalities." The final result of the vote: He did not win.

CHAPTER 23

Getting Back to Where We Began

There seems to be two main human experiences that can open us up and grab our attention, the experiences of love and suffering. Many parents say the birth of their child was truly an experience of God. It was an experience of love and joy so powerful that it took their focus off of themselves and placed their focus squarely on another human being. If we love greatly, it is fairly certain we will suffer as well because we have somehow given up control to another.

Suffering can lead us in either of two directions. We can become a better person because of the suffering, or we can become bitter and shut down. In the words of Rev. Paula Ferry Boccia, an interfaith minister and part time dean of the New Seminary in New York City:

> As we wrestle with our ego, and try to truly love another, we suffer greatly. That is the price of great love. The love that says, no matter how much you don't get it, no matter how many mistakes you make, no matter how many times you betray me, I will love you. That is the love Jesus had for us that saved us from ourselves. Jesus asks this of us

because this is what transforms and resurrects us into our True Self.

Every personal relationship in our lives, but especially our relationship with God, has the capacity and potential to move us beyond whom we think we are, to transform us, and to bring us to our true selves, our true identity in God. However, selfishness shuts down and closes us off from this possibility and potential. Fr. Richard Gula asserts that living a selfish life is dangerous and deadly:

> Now we can put our finger on what personal sin is in all its ugliness. Sin is selfishness, pure and simple. We become sinful to the extent that we turn inward, refuse to respond, and cut off the dynamic of giving and receiving love. In sin, we cease to pay attention to, or care about, anyone outside ourselves. When we sin, we destroy other people and ourselves at the same time. We destroy bonds of peace and justice, and spread conditions of fear, hatred, violence, and bring havoc into the lives of other people and into our own. (103-104)

We all have the need to be loved. We all have a need to know that we matter. Selfish behavior or attitudes are an attempt to ensure that our need to be loved is met. We are called to pay attention to others and to how our life affects them. But a person who displays selfish behavior has a call to pay attention backwards, in which the person is saying, "Pay attention to me!" We break this pattern and power of sin based on selfishness when we finally believe that we already are deeply and profoundly loved by God, and that we already matter to God.

One beautiful, sunny, and pleasant day in central

Wisconsin, two of my brothers and I decided to go fishing. It was a perfect day to be in a boat on the river. At the landing site, we backed the boat into the water, got in, and off we went floating down the river. The water was as smooth as glass, without any ripples. We enjoyed the pleasant weather and that peaceful easy feeling of being together. After a while, who knows how long, one of my brothers noticed that we had been drifting. The water was so still, we could not believe how far we had drifted.

The only way we knew that we had drifted, and were able to realize how far we had drifted, was to look back at where we put our boat in the river. We needed a reference point. We all need some point of reference in our lives. Even Jesus needed a point of reference. Jesus needed some solid truth on which He could rely. Perhaps that truth, that point of reference, came at His baptism. The Heavens broke open and a voice was heard, "This is my beloved Son, in whom I am well pleased, listen to him" (Matt. 3:17, Mk 1:11 and Luke 3:22). When Jesus stepped out of the water, He knew He was a Son, and He was a Beloved Son.

Jesus' point of reference was His identity in the Father. We also have a point of reference for our lives, and as it was for Jesus, that point of reference is who we are in terms of our relationship with God. "The first and foremost identity for (Christian) people is a child of God. Those who seek to live authentically need to know who they truly are" (Pierce, 12).

Jesus said in Luke 19:10, "The Son of Man has come to seek and to save what was lost." What do you think was lost? I believe what was lost was our true identity. We suffer because we have lost our point of reference, our true identity, our identity of who we truly are in God.

Before we did anything right or wrong, before we said or thought anything good or bad, from the first moment of our existence, God loved us. This especially is a powerful point of reference for me. It is so easy to lose sight of this truth and begin the downward spiral, and see ourselves in negative ways. We search for something or someone else to fill that void to give us an identity, and this search leaves us adrift and empty, drifting away from the truth of who we really are in God.

> We read in 1 John 3: 1-2:
>
> You must see what great love the Father has lavished on us by letting us be called God's children--which is what we are! … My dear friends, we are <u>already</u> God's children, but what we shall be in the future has not yet been revealed. We are well aware that when he appears we shall be like him, because we shall see him as he really is.

This is, in fact, who we are! When we get the "alreadys" right and fully understand and internalize the truth that we are God's children, so much would fall into proper place.

In life, it is so easy to drift or to simply go off course. Life does that to us. We easily get off track and maybe even lose our way. Events and choices in life may cause us to drift without us even realizing that we have drifted. Most of the time we are not aware of our drifting without someone or something to call our attention to this.

When the argument broke out among Jesus' disciples about which of them was the greatest, their eyes were only focused inward on themselves. Their egos had gone wild. However, Jesus knew their thoughts.   He took a simple little child and said to His disciples, "Anyone who welcomes this little child in my name welcomes me; and anyone who welcomes me, welcomes the One who sent me. The least among you is the one who is the greatest" (Matt 18: 1-5).

Yes, the example and simplicity of a little child can help us to see in a new way. One of the most moving events I have ever experienced occurred on Mother's Day, 2010. I was invited to visit a family who I had come to know and love. They have three children, a daughter in fifth grade, a son in second grade, and a four-year old son, Cade. I arrived at their home and drove into their driveway. I got out of my car and was greeted by Cade who walked up to me cradling a package in his little arms. The package was a blob of wrapping paper all taped in every direction.

"For me?" I asked. He replied in his cute little voice, "For you, Fr. Bob." "Should I open it?" "Yes sir," he replied. I did not quite know how to open it, or where to start to open it. The package was not a box, it was not a bag; the package was simply a blob of wrapping paper with scotch tape everywhere.

Finally I got it open, and in this mess of wrapping paper I found a baseball cap. A dirty, well used, and obviously adjusted to his little four-year-old sized head, baseball cap. I asked, "Cade, is this yours? This looks like one of your favorite caps." He said in his polite little way, "Yes, sir." I was deeply moved. I was speechless. I told him that I would wear it proudly, but some day I would give it back to him. He liked the sound of that, and I did eventually give the baseball cap back to him.

How sweet was that! His parents had not been able to figure out why earlier that morning Cade had asked for wrapping paper and tape. They had no idea what he had been planning to do. Even his parents could not believe their little four-year-old son's act of incredible kindness, sweetness, and his generous and giving spirit.

I will never forget that moment when I saw Cade gently and ever so slowly walk toward me cradling that precious glob of wrapping paper in his little arms. Oh, to have that childlike heart and way! Oh to have that simplicity, that gentle, generous and unselfish spirit. All egos were silenced. There was no need to prove anything to anyone. No words of theology were discussed. At that moment everything was right in the world. At that moment I could no longer find the place where God stopped and Cade began, nor where Cade stopped and God began. They were one and the same. At that moment the world was again a beautiful place.

CHAPTER 24

Learning the Lessons of Life

We all know that life produces hardships, disappointments, heartaches, heartbreaks, and all kinds of trials. We may slip into thinking that God is punishing us or that maybe God is displeased and disappointed with us, and that this could be God's way of getting even with us. But when we stand strong and rely on our point of reference, we can trust that God can use everything in our life to bring about good.

The letter to the Hebrews (Heb. 12:5-7) invites us to look upon the trials we experience throughout life, as well as the hardships and disappointments, as a means of discipline. "Do not disdain the discipline of the Lord or lose heart when reproved by Him; for whom the Lord loves, He disciplines" (NAB). We tend to associate discipline with punishment. Punishment is a response to something that happened in the past, maybe even in the last few minutes, whereas discipline is for the sake of the future, for the purpose of growth. Discipline is really an act of love, an act of caring and concern for the growth of another.

I admit, when I face some kind of difficulty, my first prayer is not, "Thank you God." My first prayer is, "God, make it go away!" However, when we believe that God is good and that God looks out for our good, we can have the courage to trust again and to pay attention and listen to our life.

The great issue or question of faith is not, "Is there a God?" or "Do I believe in God?" The great question of faith is, "Do I, can I, trust this God?" or "Can I entrust God with my life?" So much hinges on how we answer this question of trust. I know, in my case, and I believe this is a common human experience; I only fully trust those I know and love as well as those who know me and love me, those who want the best for me. If this is true, where does God fall into these categories? It is necessary to build and develop a close foundation and relationship with God. We tend not to trust strangers, so God cannot remain a stranger to us.

Jesus used the analogy of the vine and the branches (John 15: 1-11) to describe this unity and connection. Prayer becomes taking time to stay connected. This is essential to build trust with God. In this union, through our developing friendship with the Lord, we slowly discover that it is safe to risk being ourselves, to be honest, and to trust God with the stuff of our lives. We ask such questions as, "God, what are you trying to teach me through this? What do I need to learn?" Throughout, we are invited to be gentle with ourselves as God is gentle with us. Just as we learn how to pray by praying, so we learn to trust by trusting.

Several years ago, I struggled with some decisions and with a new direction of ministry that seemed to be entering my life. I really tried to seek the Spirit to help me. Finally the time came when I had to make my important decision. I consulted a fellow Franciscan. He said to me, "Bob, I have no doubt you tried to listen to the direction and promptings of the Spirit. Now that you have trusted God, would you just start trusting yourself?" I guess that is why it is called faith.

Many people say to me that they do not trust God enough. This seems to be a common feeling many of us have. However, if we have done all we can to maintain and strengthen our bond and connection with God, and we have been honest with ourselves and with God, and have listened, perhaps we then need to hear the same comment I heard, "Would you just start trusting yourself?"

Jesus revealed to us our God who chooses to relate to us as a loving Father to adult children. God wants to produce mature, responsible, stronger and better people. God wants to produce people of depth, commitment, wisdom, compassion, capable of presence, and who come to know and love themselves as they are known and loved by God. These mature qualities are what healthy religion produces.

Life is really our best spiritual teacher when we listen to what is going on in us and around us. God is as close to us as our life! We keep in mind our personal truth, our point of reference, that we are already beloved sons and daughters of God. When we pay attention to the stuff of our lives and allow it to teach us, to mature us, to "grow us up," we can believe and know God is indeed a loving Father to His adult children, to you and to me.

CHAPTER 25

Becoming the One Who Welcomes Us

Of the many parables Jesus told, the prodigal son is frequently considered one of the greatest (Luke 15: 11-32). In fact, some people say that if we forget all of Scripture and we only remember the parable of the prodigal son, we would still know the Gospel message. This parable serves as another point of reference for our lives. This parable can serve as a lens, another pair of eyeglasses, through which we more clearly see the true image of God the Father as well as our own image and who we are to become.

In this parable, the father had two sons. One son would not wait for his father's death to receive his share of his inheritance. After he received his inheritance, he wasted it on wild living. His style of living declined so low that he was hired to feed hogs and he even ate with them. When this rebellious son decided to return home from his revelry, the father saw him at a distance, ran to him, and welcomed him home. The son who never rebelled was angry about how his father welcomed his rebellious brother. The father explained that they must rejoice and celebrate his return.

One game most children play is hide and seek. It is fun to find a good spot to hide where we cannot be found. As a child, and even into my adult years, I used to think that we have a hide-and-seek God. God hides from us and we somehow have to find God. It was a game God played with us. But I now realize I had it backwards. God was not hiding from me; I was hiding from God.

When we come out of hiding and let ourselves be found by God, we will not be met with a finger-shaking God, but by a God whose eternal stance is arms wide open ready to embrace and welcome us home. In the parable of the prodigal son, when the younger son returned to the father, the father did not even demand an explanation. No explanation was necessary. All that mattered to the father was that his son was back; his son was with him, and he was with his son! This is mercy, this is grace, and this is the message of the Gospel. How important this parable is for us! As one preacher simply put it, "If it's not the Gospel of grace, it's not the Gospel."

There is a story about a young man who lived a portion of his life as a runaway. When he settled down, he was asked, "When you were on the run, what were you looking for? What did you want?" He answered, "I wanted someone to care enough to come looking for me." Jesus assures us through the parable of the prodigal son that this is what God is like! God is like this!

Throughout the years, I questioned whether I was like the younger son or the elder son in the parable of the prodigal son. I have come to realize that I am a little of both. However, after reading the book, *The Return of the Prodigal Son: A Meditation on Fathers, Brothers, and Sons*, Henri Nouwen coaxed me to take my focus off the two sons and focus on the father.

Nouwen's insight changed my entire view of this parable. Before reading his book, I thought the ultimate goal of our spiritual lives and journey was to come home to the Father; however, that is only the beginning. Nouwen wrote, "… my final vocation is indeed to *become like the Father* and to live out his divine compassion in my daily life. Though I am both the younger son and the elder son, I am not to remain them, but to become the Father (114).

Nouwen points out there has to be more to our spiritual journey than being a son or a daughter who repeatedly and endlessly returns to the Father for forgiveness. Nouwen states, "I am destined to step into the place of my Father and offer to others the same compassion that the Father has offered me. The return to the Father is ultimately the challenge to *become the Father*" (116). But, "Do I want to be like the father? Do I want to be, not just the one who is being forgiven, but also the one who forgives; not just the one who is being welcomed home, but also the one who welcomes home; not just the one who receives compassion, but the one who offers it as well" (115). For Nouwen, "Becoming like the heavenly Father is not just one important aspect of Jesus' teaching, it is the very heart of his message" (116-117).

If our spiritual life is to lead us to become the father, who will guide us there, and what could be a stumbling block to this path? The largest stumbling block to the spiritual path to become the father is our own image of the Father. If we consider God threatening, eager to punish and watching our every misstep and mistake, we will keep God at a careful distance while, at the same time, long for God's blessing and intimacy.

Nouwen calls this fear of God one of the great human tragedies in that this fear has paralyzed the mental and emotional lives of many people. Nouwen writes, "The final stage of the spiritual life is to so fully let go of all fear of the Father that it becomes possible to become like him. As long as the Father evokes fear, the Father remains an outsider and cannot dwell within me" (114).

Our ultimate guide and model to become the father is the true Son of the Father, Jesus. Jesus said, "I am the way, and the truth and the life; no one comes to the Father but through me. If you really knew me, you would know my Father also" (John 14: 6-7). Unfortunately, Christian people often misinterpret this passage of Scripture, the part that states, "… no one comes to the Father, but through me." This passage is often misinterpreted to mean that only those who believe in Jesus are saved or, in other words, are eligible for heaven or heaven-bound, to the exclusion of all other people.

Jesus is the true revelation of the Father. Is it possible that the whole point of Jesus' life was to reveal to us human beings finally and forever what God is really like? "Long ago God spoke to our ancestors in many and various ways by the prophets, but in these last days he has spoken to us by the Son … He is the reflection of God's glory and the exact imprint of God's very being" (Heb. 1:1-3). We come to *know* the Father through the Son. By following the Gospel of Jesus Christ, Christian people who say they follow Jesus and profess Jesus to be their Lord and Savior should display, reveal and model God whom Jesus called God and Father, and make the Christian way of life attractive and attract others by the way they live, by what they say and what they do. The way of Jesus is not so much about a set of beliefs; it is about a way of life.

Jesus came to make the Father known to us and to all humanity. Jesus prayed, "Father, the world does not know you, but I know you; and these know that you have sent me. I made your name known to them, and I will make it known, so that the love with which you have loved me may be in them, and I in them" (John 17: 25-26).

We are to continue this ministry, mission and message of Jesus to make God known. We are to keep alive this truth of God, this vision of God that Jesus taught and lived. This mission is too big for any one individual, and we cannot do this on our own. This mission needs a church, a community of believers who support and challenge one another to keep our eyes and focus on the big picture, the Kingdom of God, God's vision for our world. I like the following definition of a Christian community:

Christian community itself is a new, distinct human possibility, which will exist only if men and women freely decide to follow Jesus together. Christian community is different from other human gatherings because it is comprised of people who know they are sinners, who believe they are loved, and thus who have no reason to be afraid. (Reiser, 27)

Followers of Jesus are given something all human beings crave, a sense of purpose and a sense of mission. All followers of Jesus are naturally "mission-minded." In *Beyond the Mirror*, Nouwen writes, "I understand now that 'making known' is not primarily a question of words, arguments, language, and methods. What is at stake here is a way that tries less to persuade than to <u>demonstrate</u>. It is the way of witness" (59). While being a Christian is a great privilege, it is even more a tremendous responsibility. People of other religions, even non-believers should be able to look at Christians and say, "That is what God is like! God is like that!"

CHAPTER 26

Being with the One Who Is with Us

We are all on a journey. We come from God, and we return to God. While this journey is called spiritual, the real goal is to become a better human being, to become more Christ-like, or as Nouwen asserts, to become the father.

When I was about 32 years old, my Dad told me a heartwarming story, a bit of his spiritual journey. He invited me to go for a walk with him, and as we neared the end of our driveway, he said, "I have something to tell you, but you're going to think I'm crazy." I told him that I wanted to hear what he had to say. He said, "I am already in my mid sixties, and I don't know how much longer I have to live. So I've been wondering how I stand with God at this time of my life."

Dad began to tell me his story. "I decided to take a nap one day. It was around the middle of the afternoon. I don't think I was really sleeping. A voice called me in a loud whisper, 'My boy! My boy!' I looked up, and saw a bright light from above coming down from the ceiling. The bright light continued to descend and come closer. The bright light turned into a Scripture page filled with writing. The edges of the page were old and somewhat yellowed and tattered. I couldn't read the writing on the page, but I could read the writing on the bottom of the page. The writing spelled out, 'As you abide with me, so also I abide with you.' The page turned into a bright light again, ascended, and disappeared."

As my Dad got to this point of the story, he was clearly emotional and teary-eyed. He spoke with such humility, with such deep gratitude and love for God. He was overwhelmed by the experience. I was not only deeply moved by his story, but also by his emotion and the way he described his experience. I did not know what to say. My Dad continued, "I didn't know what to do with what happened to me. Do I dare tell your Mom?"

My Dad then told me something that I will never forget and for which I am eternally grateful to God. He said, "After that experience in the afternoon, later that day, Mom and I were in the barn and it was time to milk the cows. I was at one end of the barn and Mom was at the other end. She walked over to me, and asked me, "Did God ever whisper in your ear?" My Dad told me that he was startled and didn't know what to say. Finally, my Dad said to her, "Why would you ever ask such a question?" She said, "I was just standing there, and this question came into my head. I couldn't get it out of my mind, so I had to come and ask you." Dad told her the entire story, his whole experience. They ended up in each other's embrace. I thought how good of God to include my mother in this way which gave my Dad the courage, the opportunity and opening to share his experience with Mom.

I will never forget the message and answer to Dad's question to God, "Where do I stand with you, God?" *As you abide with me, so also I abide with you.* Earlier in this book, I wrote that we are invited to live our life from the Life that lives within us. It is the language of relationship, the language of union, communion and mutual indwelling.

When I see a daisy, I remember as a young child picking each petal off the flower and each time saying, "She loves me; she loves me not." We do this with God. "God loves me; God loves me not. God loves me more today; I do not think God loves me so much today." We constantly check our "God meter" to see if we are important to God today. The truth is we always deeply matter to God. God cannot love you more than God is loving you right now. How I wish I would live in this truth all the time! In my better moments, I do.

I hope at times we can be like children, astonished, amazed, filled with wonder, content and secure in the knowledge that it is enough to simply be son or daughter to the Father and allow the Father simply to be Father to us. We can put away our ego for a while and say, "Isn't God something!" rather than "Aren't we something!" At those moments when everything seems too good to be true, we may even be moved to say, "God, you must have me confused with someone else." We cannot afford to lose this dimension of Christianity! St. Francis did not change until he was changed by his relationship with God, and then he changed the world.

CHAPTER 27

Going with the Flow

We cannot win God's love, and neither can we lose God's love. But we are free to receive God's love or not. At a religious service with elementary students, I asked the children what are some ways we follow Jesus. I received the usual answers: "Do my chores, do my homework, obey my parents, be nice to my little sister, feed the dog." After a number of children responded, a young boy in the second or third grade raised his hand. I looked at him and asked, "Yes, how do you think we can follow Jesus?" He said, "*Think of Him.*" I was so moved by this child's answer.

I immediately wondered what God was doing in that young boy. Many people are not even aware of what I call the "inner life." Truly this young boy had a relationship with the Lord and the relationship was mutual. His answer stopped me in my tracks. I wanted to stop and let that answer settle into my heart and soul.

This young boy lived in the flow of life and love; his life and his following of Jesus flowed from that relationship. His Christian life was a response to what was happening in him. We do not *earn* God's love; we *return* God's love.

Nature provides an image to help us picture how our Christian life is a response. In his book, *Gratefulness, the*

Heart of Prayer, Brother David Steindl-Rast writes that winter had released its tight grip and gave way to the season of spring. He continues:

> If ever one feels what a blessing warm
> sunshine can be, it is after a long winter in the
> Austrian Alps. Every foot of ground seems
> to feel that blessing. And there, stomping
> through a soggy bottom, suddenly we
> children stood before the first flowers. All
> these flowers, no bigger than a nickel, each on
> its own sturdy stem, were the blessing earth
> sent up in answer [response] to the blessing
> coming down from the sun. Looking at this
> colorful array of flowers, I simply saw it,
> walked into it, became it, as my eyes blessed
> God." (79-80)

When we peer into the lives of the saints, we seldom hear how much they loved God. Rather the saints emphasize their overwhelming experience of how much God loved them. The saints lived in ways that tried to give back in response to the initial and never-ending acceptance and love that they experienced from God. We usually answer the question, "How do we know we love God?" with this answer, "By our quality and quantity of love for neighbor." For the saints, the answer would be the same. However the question could be, "How do we know we believe God loves us?"

God says to us, "I love you; love me back." God loves us first, accepts us first, and in response, that love makes demands on our life. Love and acts of service are the responsibility of everyone for which there are no exceptions, young and old, rich and poor alike, and everyone in between.

What is true for us is true for everyone. Being chosen

by God does not mean that everyone else is not chosen. We experience being chosen so we can help others to believe and experience that they are chosen. We are special in the eyes of God so we can help others discover they are special in the eyes to God as well. When we discover our identity as sons and daughters of God, we help others discover that they too are beloved sons and daughters of the living God.

Can you imagine a world where everyone's daily mission is to help others to see and discover for themselves that they are already beloved children of God, special, chosen and loved beyond measure? Can you imagine a world like that? How different our world would look! What would this world look like? It would look like the Kingdom of God, the Kingdom Jesus came to proclaim, model, and even died trying to bring about. Maybe that is one way we can bring heaven closer to earth and earth closer to heaven, which is a good way to describe the Kingdom.

We always want Jesus to hear and answer our prayers. But our relationship with the Lord is a two-way relationship. It is not just what we want Jesus to do for us, but also what Jesus wants us to do for Him. In John 17:20-23, we hear a prayer by Jesus in which He prays for us. "Father, I pray that they may be one in us … so the world will know that you sent me, and that you love them as you loved me." God needs useable people as His instruments to reflect the nature of God to our world. God looks for "images and likenesses" of who God is.

Even though the language for God in our Bible is primarily male, or masculine, we know that God is beyond gender. I use masculine language in this book simply to be consistent. Also, the pronouns of our English language, him and her, he and she, only refer to one gender, and exclude the other. These pronouns are unable to contain or express both the masculine and feminine quality of God.

Isaiah, the prophet, opens our imagination and expands our image of God. Isa. 42:14 describes God giving birth to the people; Isa. 49:15-16 depicts God like a mother, who would never forget her child; Isa. 66:10-14 portrays God as a nursing mother who bounces her infant on her lap and who comforts and takes delight in her child. We have a God strong enough to be gentle and gentle enough to be strong.

I have heard many times that we are to see Jesus in everyone. I honestly admit that this is very difficult for me and not because I do not believe it. While seeing Jesus in everyone is difficult for me for reasons I do not know, I do believe that each and every person is a beloved son or daughter of God. A speaker at a conference said that after he gave the keynote address, a woman came to him and began to speak angrily about God. As she talked, he was becoming angry with her. He had just given a speech about the God of love, mercy and forgiveness. He was ready to interrupt her, to stop her, and then he said he heard a little voice in his ear say, "Just love her. She's mine already; she just doesn't know it yet."

After that corrective word from the Spirit, he stood with her and listened as she described the horrible events of her life. Slowly her heart softened and opened. She just needed to vent her frustration to someone who would actually take the time to pay attention to her and to listen to her. When we are with others, can we hear that same message, "Just love them. They are mine already; they just don't know it yet!"

I know as a minister, I can talk "until I am blue in the face and ready to pass out" about how much God loves us, but most will not hear the message. I understand why this is so. People have a hard time believing it because they have experienced very little actual love from others. Yet Jesus commanded us to love. Jesus did not say wait until we get healed, then love; wait until we grow up, then love; wait until we get it together and have dealt with all our wounds and scars, then love.

Where God's love for us and our love for God intersect, it is there that our lives truly bear fruit. If Jesus makes a difference in our lives, we will make a difference in the lives of others. When the commandment to love God and the commandment to love our neighbor come together, Jesus says, "We are not far from the Kingdom" (Mark 12:34).

CONCLUSION

St. John of the Cross was a religious order priest and mystic in the sixteenth century. Many years ago I had written a quote from St. John of the Cross that I wanted to remember, of which I do not know the source. He wrote, "I realized that at the end, our lives shall not be judged on the number and intensity of our religious experiences nor on the graces of prayer which we have received — but on LOVE alone."

Love is the goal of ALL RELIGION(S). Being human and being religious have to happen together. If our religion does not lead us to an increase of receiving and giving love, could we not consider that religion to be "misleading," or religion lived poorly? St. Paul, in his famous "love chapter" (1 Cor. 13), which is often read at wedding ceremonies, writes with deep self reflection and great humility:

> If I speak with human tongues and angelic as well, but do not have love, I am a noisy gong, a clanging cymbal. If I have the gift of prophecy and, with full knowledge, comprehend all mysteries, if I have faith great enough to move mountains, but have not love, I am nothing. (vs. 1-2)

This same principle that St. Paul wrote also applies to me at this time. If I can do this and do that and everything else, *even if I should write a book*, but have not love, I am nothing and all this accounts for nothing.

One Sunday I was privileged to listen to another priest preach. He said that the greatest hunger we have is our hunger for God. I had heard this message many times. I am sure you have, too. But this time I found myself asking, "What does that mean? What is this hunger that not just you and I, but all humanity hungers for?" The greatest need we have as human beings is to love and be loved. Only God can truly satisfy this hunger in the human heart. We are invited to know God as revealed in Jesus, to be in relationship with God, but also, even more importantly, to know that we are known by God.

My hope is that we, somehow, know how much we are loved by God, the One who loved us first. My hope is that we might see ourselves as God sees us, that we know ourselves as we are known, and that we love ourselves as we are loved. This truth, this reality, changes just about everything. When we are filled with this truth, a truth that seems too good to be true, we may be compelled to say, "God, you must have me confused with someone else."

We are humbled and all we can say to God is, "Thank you, God." God says to us in return, "You are welcome. Thank you!" We say to God, "God, I love you." God says to us, "I love you too!" This is what we hunger for! I am convinced this is what we hunger for when we say we hunger for God. We hunger to know that we are known by God and that we actually matter to God.

Several years ago I visited a woman who suffered from cancer and was under hospice care in her home. Every time I visited her, no matter what her husband was doing, he stopped and we both went into the bedroom to be with her. I could hear, see, and sense the immense love in that room between this husband and wife. I came to her bedside and greeted her. Even in the final stage of her life, she was always sparkly-eyed, sporting a delightful and contagious smile. It was so easy to be with her and her husband, and hard to leave, simply because of the love that flowed between them, sometimes through words, sometimes through silence when words were not necessary.

When she passed away, I officiated at her funeral. Several weeks later, I stopped by their house to visit the husband, now a widower. He spoke of his love for his deceased wife and how much he missed her. He told me that he was going through some things in the house after she died and found a card that she had written to him, her last card to him before she got sick. His wife had written, "I am blessed with the greatest blessing one can have: to love someone with all my heart who also loves me."

"God is love, and those who abide in love abide in God, and God in them" (1 John 4:16).

Appendix

Let Us Pray

Where do we go from here? Looking at our world as it is today, while we see much grace, goodness and generosity, there are many cases of "man's inhumanity to man" as Robert Burns said in his poem, *Man Was Made to Mourn: A Dirge*. Every direction we look, whether worldwide, nationally, or even within our workplaces, homes and families, we have economic, relational, and political problems and conflicts. However, I contend our problem is PRIMARILY A SPIRITUAL PROBLEM. Does this sound too simplistic or naïve?

There are definitely some things we need to stop doing; there are some things we need to *start* doing. In biblical language, this means to repent. Do you think everything would suddenly change if we posted the Ten Commandments on the doorpost of every home, on the bulletin boards of every school, on every street corner, and on the walls inside every civic and religious building?

I wish simply posting the Ten Commandments everywhere would change behavior and attitudes that are detrimental or destructive to our society. However, nothing much will change on the outside if we remain the same on the inside. "Then [Jesus] called the crowd again and said to them, 'Let anyone with ears to hear, listen. For it is from within, from the human heart, that evil intentions come'" (Mark 7: 14, 21). A woman who walked more than 25,000 miles on a personal pilgrimage of peace and called herself the "Peace Pilgrim" (1908-1981) expressed this same principle: "World peace will never be stable until enough of us find inner peace to stabilize it." The Spirit changes us from the inside out and helps us to "see" in a new way.

What would happen if we really believed that we are indeed God's beloved children, God's beloved sons and daughters, and our self-perception and actions flowed from this truth? It is crucial that we do not lose sight of this truth, our true identity. We would be compelled to return the compliment to others, to treat others with this same dignity, to help them to see this truth for themselves, and then maybe our acts of inhumanity would stop.

We have a SPIRITUAL PROBLEM. Isaiah, in the name of God, wrote, "For MY thoughts are not your thoughts, nor are MY ways your ways, says the Lord" (Isa. 55:8). We can either follow the ways of Jesus, or we can *get in the way*. As Jesus challenged Peter when Jesus predicted his own suffering and death, "Peter, you are thinking, not as God does, but as human beings do" (Mark 8:33).

How do we think and act not as God does, but as human beings do? We say, "Might makes right; only the strongest survive; watch out for number one" and in many cases, we still believe in an eye-for-an-eye.

We have divided our world into winners and losers, right and left, progressives and conservatives. We have allowed this same divisive language to seep into our thinking as Christians and even into the Church, and at times to overwhelm and silence the Scriptures. There is only one message we follow, the message of the Gospel which cuts through the divisive language.

The truth is, we have ALL SINNED and fallen short. We are all a part of "where we are," responsible for the present conditions of our world, for good or for ill. Where do we go from here? What do we pray? Do we pray, "God, I thank you that I am not like other people?" (Luke 18:11).

When one side simply continues to blame, criticize or accuse the other for that which they themselves have done, this gets us nowhere. We cannot scapegoat and thereby force a person or a group to bear all the blame or suffering, or quickly demonize others while denying our own wrongdoing. "How can you see the speck in another's eye, and ignore the log in your own?" (Matt 7:3-5).

I have come to the point that when I look at our world, country, society, and Church today, all I can really pray is "*Have mercy on us, and on the whole world.*" What else can we pray? We have ALL SINNED and fallen short.

I am heartened when I look at history and see the role that prayer played. In an article entitled "Prayer and Revival," J. Edwin Orr (1912-1987), a revival historian, recounts three "great awakenings" in American history and their subsequent social impact. Orr begins his article with this statement: "Dr. A.T. Pierson once said, "There has never been a spiritual awakening in any country or locality that did not begin in united prayer." These awakenings, these revivals, were initiated and energized through a "concert of prayer," a movement of prayer. I do not know what else we can humbly and honestly pray at this time except "*Have mercy on us and on the whole world.*"

There is a prayer for Divine Mercy, also known as the Chaplet of Divine Mercy, that expresses our littleness and helplessness as well as our trust and loving surrender in light of the enormity of God's mercy. This prayer for mercy is also a *lament* by which we can prayerfully admit that often our ways are not God's ways, that we are thinking and acting not as God does, and, in turn, that we too readily lose sight of who we truly are.

Through Sister Mary Faustina (1905-1938), who is known as the apostle of Divine Mercy, the Lord Jesus communicated to the world this great message and prayer for God's mercy. He revealed the pattern of Christian life based on a child-like trust in God and on the attitude of mercy toward one's neighbor.

This prayer of Mercy was recorded live in a church in Baton Rouge, Louisiana, and is available at the following website: **bkonopa.blogspot.com**; then click on the YouTube address. Through this live recording you will join more than six hundred people in the church in a concert of prayer. If you want a more professional rendition and recording, I recommend that you go to the website **divinemercyinsong. com** where you can listen to a sampling of this sung prayer for Divine Mercy and order the CD.

As we learned from the parable of the prodigal son, Jesus' call and challenge to us is to ultimately become like the Father. Are we there yet? Are we even moving in that direction? As we look at the present conditions and our reality around us, let us pray this prayer of MERCY and create a *concert of prayer,* a prayer that is honest and humble. What else can we pray?

If you wish to personally comment about this book, please email:

whatIwasmissing@gmail.com

References

Boccia, M., and Boccia, P.F. "*Thy Kingdom Come, My Kingdom Go*," *Radical Grace*. 22.3 (Jul-Sept 2009).

Borg, M.J. *The Heart of Christianity: Rediscovering a Life of Faith*. New York: HarperCollins Publishers, 2003.

Christenson, E. *Lord, Change Me!* Wheaton: Victor Books, 1979.

Gray, Donald P. *Jesus, the Way to Freedom*. Winona: St. Mary's College Press, 1979.

Gula, R.M., S.S. *To Walk Together Again: The Sacrament of Reconciliation*." Ramsey: Paulist Press, 1984.

Ingham, M.B., C.S.J. *Rejoicing in the Works of the Lord: Beauty in the Franciscan Tradition*." St. Bonaventure University: Franciscan Institute, 2009.

Kennedy, E. *If You Really Knew Me, Would You Still Like Me?* Niles: Argus Communications, 1975.

Manning, B. *A Stranger to Self-Hatred: A Glimpse of Jesus*. Denville: Dimension Books, Inc., 1982.

Nouwen, H., J.M. *Beyond the Mirror: Reflections on Life and Death*. New York: Crossroad Publishing Company, 2001.

Nouwen, H., J.M. *The Return of the Prodigal Son: A Meditation on Fathers, Brothers, and Sons*. New York: Doubleday, 1992.

Peck, M.S., M.D. *People of the Lie: The Hope for Healing Human Evil.* New York: Simon & Schuster, Inc., 1983.

Pierce, G., F.A. *The World as It Should Be: Living Authentically in the Here-and-Now Kingdom of God.* Chicago: Loyola Press, 2010.

Powell, J., S.J. *Why am I Afraid to Tell You Who I Am?* Valencia: Tabor Publishing, 1969.

Reiser, W.E., S.J. *Drawn to the Divine: A Spirituality of Revelation.* Notre Dame: Ave Maria Press, 1987.

Rohlheiser, R. *Does God Have Favorites?* Sept. 19, 2010.

Rohlheiser, R. *Love in a Time of Opposition.* July 25, 2010.

Rohr, R. *Things Hidden: Scripture as Spirituality.* Cincinnati: St. Anthony Messenger Press, 2008.

Steindl-Rast, D. *Gratefulness, the Heart of Prayer: An Approach to Life in Fullness.* Mahwah: Paulist Press, 1984.

Walsh, E. *The Ministry of the Celebrating Community.* Glendale: Pastoral Arts Associates of North America, 1977.

bethquick.com, sermon 3-2-08, Cycle A.

Bible quotations, unless otherwise noted, are from the *New Revised Standard Version of the Bible*, ©1989 by the Division of Christian Education of the National Council of Churches of Christ in the U.S.A. Used by permission. All rights reserved.

The New Jerusalem Bible. (1985). New York: Doubleday, a division of Bantam Doubleday Dell Publishing Group, Inc.

The New American Bible. (2001). Washington DC: Confraternity of Christian Doctrine, Inc.